A Jewish Savior
Through
Gentile Eyes

A Jewish Savior Through Gentile Eyes

Studies in the Gospel of Luke

RUBEL SHELLY

20th Century Christian
2809 Granny White Pike
Nashville, Tennessee 37204

Table of Contents

How Goes the War?
The decisive event in spiritual conflict: the cross

Gloomy Gus Was *Not* an Apostle
Joyous discipleship as a theme in Luke's Gospel

Chapter 1

He Belongs to All of Us

Each of the four Gospels has its own distinctive character.

Matthew is decidedly the Jewish Gospel. It opens with a "record of the genealogy of Jesus Christ, son of David, son of Abraham" (Matt. 1:1). How much more Jewish can one get? From this point of departure, Matthew develops the thesis that *Jesus of Nazareth is Israel's Messiah and the King over God's Kingdom.* Thus the first Gospel is written by a Jewish man to a Jewish audience about a Jewish theme.

Mark has a different audience. The man John Mark (cf. Acts 12:12,25; 15:37-38; Col. 4:10) spent his later life as a close associate of Peter. During that extended time with the fisherman-apostle, the younger man wrote what one early Christian dubbed "the memoirs of Peter." Mark must have heard his mentor preach these stories again and again to the racially mixed (i.e., Jew and Gentile) church at Rome. Jesus is portrayed in his Gospel, in good Roman fashion, as a man of action who is intent on fulfilling God's purpose. Mark presents the man from Nazareth as *the Suffering Servant of God*, and his theme is that "the Son of Man did not come to be served, but to serve, and to give his life a ransom for many" (Mark 10:45).

Skipping the third Gospel for the time being, John is unique among the church's four early faith-tracts about Jesus. The first three are typically called "the synoptic (i.e., common-view) Gospels." John stands alone, however, in writing a reflective and deeply theological account of the life of Jesus. He is less concerned about a travel narrative with precise sequencing of events than to declare that *Jesus is the Source of Life* (John 1:4). The explicit purpose of the book is to lead people to believe on Jesus for the sake of having "life in his name" (John 20:30-31).

The Gospel of Luke

Returning now to the third Gospel, Luke has its distinctives, too. It is the Gospel to the Gentiles. The only one of the Gospels written by a Greek, it is addressed to the Greek mind. It is for people who do not know Jewish literature, idioms, and figures of speech (cf. Matt. 24:15; Luke 21:20). Thus there is very little quoting of the Old Testament. Luke's target audience would neither know nor accept at face value the sacred writings of Israel.

The man Luke didn't write, then, in the style of Matthew. Nor did he put the same slant on Jesus' life and activities that Mark did in writing for people around the Roman Empire's capital city. And he didn't use the heavily theological style that John would later employ.

Luke accepted a Spirit-led task of writing a narrative account of the life and teaching of Jesus for the larger Roman world of his day. It was an exercise in trans-cultural communication to interpret the significance of a Jewish Messiah-Redeemer-King to a non-Jewish audience. He was looking for "selling points" about Jesus which would allow people with a background radically different from life in first-century Palestine to understand and believe on him as the Son of God.

Out of his personal attempt to see this Jewish Savior through his Gentile eyes, Luke produced a piece of sacred literature which affirms that Jesus belongs to Jew and Gentile alike. According to Dr. Luke, *Jesus belongs to all of us*.

Luke was from a class very unlikely to be drawn to Jesus. Remember Paul's admission that not many edu-cated, influential, or high-ranking people of the first century belonged to the church of God (cf. 1 Cor. 1:26)? Luke was one of the exceptions. He was apparently an educated man who committed his better-than-average gifts to the spread of the story of Jesus Christ.

Most everything we know about the man Luke can be summed up in a few lines. That he was a Gentile is known from Paul's distinction of some men who were "the only Jews" working with him at the time as opposed to another group which included Luke (Col. 4:11ff). He was a medical doctor (Col. 4:14). He travelled with Paul intermittently during the missionary tours of the apostle and was with him during the latter's two-year imprisonment at Rome (Phile. 24). He was still with Paul at the end of the great apostle's career and life (2 Tim. 4:11).

The quality of his writing proves that Luke was a literate man. Not only did he know the science and medicine of his time, but he also knew the language. Thus his Gospel has some of the most beautiful sections of Greek prose that survive to us from any first-century source. Renan pronounced Luke's Gospel "the most beautiful book in the world."

Luke obviously believed that there were other people in the world of his time who would be thrilled to know about the Jewish Messiah who was Lord of all. Savior of Jews and Gentiles alike. Sovereign of all humanity. So he set about to write an account of Jesus. No, he was selected by the Holy Spirit to write an account of Jesus. He wrote as the Spirit moved him and produced a marvelous document of faith.

The Gospel of Luke is a companion volume to Acts of the Apostles. Acts 1:1-5 unquestionably looks back to the third Gospel. This two-volume history of the beginnings of Christianity is therefore unique. No other Gospel has a sequel. The two books taken together constitute more of the total words of the New Testament than any other writer's collection, including the epistles of Paul, and make Luke the man who wrote more of the New Testament than anyone else.

Both the Gospel and Acts are addressed to Theophilus (Luke 1:3; Acts 1:1). Though addressed to an individual, the two books are intended for public consumption. This was a common literary device of the time.

That Luke the physician wrote the Luke-Acts materials is a deduction from the so-called "we-sections" of Acts (Acts 16:10-17; 20:5-21:18; 27:1-28:16). By a process of elimination, he is the only reasonable candidate for authorship. The tradition of the early church uniformly confirms this.

Hearts from every quarter rejoice over Jesus. Illiterate peasants and physician-historians. Itinerant farm workers and established company executives. Well-heeled North Americans and poverty-stricken Latin Americans. Aching hearts beat in chests of all colors and classes of people.

People who are wealthy hurt just like people who are poor. People who live in mansions can be just as unhappy and their lives just as broken as their counterparts who live in rat-infested slums or who roam the streets. Sin is no respecter of persons, and people from all strata of society need the same thing. All of us need a Savior.

Luke's "Selling Points"

The statement was made earlier in this chapter that Luke sought "selling points" for presenting Jesus to his readers. That term is not intended to be irreverent (to Jesus) or disrespectful (of Luke). It simply affirms what all of us know about communication. Common points of interest and concern must be found between the speaker/writer and the target audience. Politicians know it. Salesmen know it. And competent Christian evangelists know it, too.

Luke was a most competent Christian evangelist. His Gospel was an exercise in trans-cultural communication. As a Gentile devotee to a religion "born from the womb of Judaism," Luke sought to bridge the gap of communication between the two worlds. From the subculture of faith, he attempted to attract unbelievers' attention to Jesus.

Some of the key themes Luke explored in his well-crafted treatise are still critical for the task of trans-cultural communication of the gospel message. If we succeed in reaching out to unbelievers from our own subculture of faith (and Christian discipleship is a subculture in our world!), we would do well to develop some of these same themes.

Luke wrote a lot about *women*. He has more to say about women than any other of the Gospel writers, more than the other three put together. Our culture needs to know that Jesus looks on women differently from the way some chauvinistic, male-dominated, conservative, religious folk look at them. Women have dignity and worth, and they have an important place in Jesus' ministry.

Luke was interested in *children* in a world that placed very little value on them. When children were being put to death at birth because of handicaps and when they were being abused by adults, Luke wrote of the gentleness of Jesus with them. In a world which is sometimes violent with its children, we would do well to both teach about and model the love of Jesus for them.

Luke was interested in the theme of *joy*. He lived in a first-century world that was rather doleful because its religions and philosophy had run against a brick wall of skepticism and could do nothing to give men and women a faith for which it could both live and die. The pervasive gloom and pessimism of our own age could stand to hear about the joy of Christ.

Luke wrote about *repentance*. Our world certainly needs to hear this theme. He wrote about *Jesus' compassion for outcasts*, the poor, the sick, and the disenfranchised. In successive chapters of this book, we will explore these and other themes of the Gospel of Luke. We will discover their historical relevance to Luke's world. And we will explore their appropriateness to our own time and situation.

No wonder the Holy Spirit selected Luke to write a faith-tract about Jesus. He had a dream for taking the story of Jesus out of a tiny little subculture and presenting him to the whole wide world. We can learn from him.

The Subject of Universalism

A fundamental emphasis which pervades the third Gospel is *universalism*. This term, as applied to Luke's writings, does not refer to the modern doctrine that all will somehow be saved in spite of themselves. It refers instead to God's offer to save all people without respect of persons. To quote from Peter as recorded in the second volume of Luke's two-volume work, it is an affirmation that "God does not show favoritism but accepts men from every nation who fear him and do what is right" (Acts 10:34b-35).

One cannot get past the opening paragraph of this Gospel without encountering distinct pointers to the comprehensive reach of the love of God.

> Many have undertaken to draw up an account of the things that have been fulfilled among us, just as they were handed down to us by those who from the first were eyewitnesses and servants of the word. Therefore, since I myself have carefully investigated everything from the beginning, it seemed good also to me to write an orderly account for you, most excellent Theophilus, so that you may know the certainty of the things you have been taught (Luke 1:1-4).

Thus begins a manuscript from a Greek physician to a Gentile acquaintance who may well have been a government official in the Roman system (*kratistos* = "most excellent," cf. Acts 23:26; 24:3; 26:25). If a bit of paraphrase can be permitted, Luke opens this way: "I want to tell you about a Jew. Now don't be turned off. I know about anti-Semitism. I also know that the Jewish region of Palestine is just a little hole-in-the-wall spot to this larger Roman Empire of ours. But I've studied this carefully. I've done research. I've taken meticulous notes, and I've put together something that I think is worth your time in reading, most excellent Theophilus. Jesus is heaven's adequacy for all of our inadequacies."

This theme is on practically every page of the Gospel of Luke. In telling of the birth of Jesus, for example, he found it significant to record how that birth was announced by angels to shepherds. "The angel said to them, 'Do not be afraid. I bring you good news of great joy that will be for all the people'" (2:10). It was not merely good news "to every Israelite" but "for *all* the people." Then, only a few lines later, the song of the heavenly host is recorded. It exults in the spiritual peace God was making possible through Christ to the residents not only of Palestine but of the whole Earth (2:14).

Still in the second chapter of Luke, Jesus is carried up to Jerusalem. There he is identified by the Holy Spirit to the prophet Simeon. Luke recorded this comment from Simeon about Jesus: "He is a light for revelation to the Gentiles" (2:32).

Only a chapter later, the ministry of John the Baptist is the topic at hand. As he wrote about the prophet who was Jesus' forerunner, Luke saw the baptizer's work among Jews as a preparation for the Messiah's task of showing salvation to all mankind. Thus, as he quoted from Isaiah 40, he used the very same lines Matthew used of John and Jesus. But it is more than a coincidence that Luke quotes five more lines than Matthew does. Why? Because Luke is concerned to get this line in before stopping: "And all mankind will see God's salvation." It wasn't as important to Matthew to

15

stress that point, for he was writings to Jews. For Luke, though, it was significant that even Jewish Scripture said Jesus was coming to "all mankind" (3:1-6).

When Matthew the Jew traced the genealogy of Jesus, he traced it back through King David to Father Abraham. But when Luke the World Citizen traced it, he went beyond Abraham and traced it to Adam (3:38).

In telling of Jesus' preaching in his hometown of Nazareth, Luke found it interesting that Jesus would point out God's willingness to bless Gentiles. Thus, in the days of a famine in the land of the Israelites, "Elijah was not sent to any of them, but to a widow in Zarephath in the region of Sidon" (4:26). Furthermore, although there were "many in Israel with leprosy" during the days of the prophet Elisha, "yet not one of them was cleansed -- only Naaman the Syrian" (4:27). Do you have to wonder why these things were significant to Luke? Why he included them in his Gospel?

Of the four Gospels, only Luke has Jesus commending members of the despised Samaritan race (cf. 10:30-37; 17:11-19). Luke consistently emphasized Jesus' concern for people that others ignored. Thus Luke shows him accepting the poor and the sick, anyone who will come to him.

One can almost go page by page through this book and find the same joyous truth highlighted. Jesus saves everyone! Jews, yes. But Gentiles also. His heart is big enough to accept all who want to be accepted.

The Practical Meaning of Universalism

What does it mean to us for Luke to present Jesus this way? What does it mean for us to truly believe Luke's thesis that Jesus belongs to all of us?

For one thing, *it has certain implications for evangelism.* Luke closes his Gospel with an account of the Great Commission. It has Jesus telling his apostles that "repentance and forgiveness of sins will be preached . . . to all nations, beginning at Jerusalem" (24:27). It will start there, but it is not to be contained there. The saving message of God's Suffering Servant is for all the nations.

Today's Christians must come to the vision that the gospel is for all. It is not just for the "Bible Belt." It is not an American possession to be shared among people who are comfortable being in each other's homes. We dare not be provincial with the saving message of God's work in Christ.

The Gospel is for people from cultures so different from ours that we would feel terribly uncomfortable going to them. Asians, Europeans, Africans. Eskimos, Poles, Brazilians. Communists, capitalists, socialists. He really does belong to all of us.

Scholars who write about Luke's two volumes often use the German term *Heilsgeschichte* (i.e., "salvation history") to signify its subject matter. The Gospel tells what Jesus began in his personal ministry, and the Acts relates the early church's effort to expand that work. The "salvation history" of millions is still waiting to be written, however, and that work requires the involvement of people who write and read Bible study books such as this one. Evangelism is not optional for Christ's people.

A second practical application of Luke's insight about the universalism of Christian faith is *compassion*. Through the writings of Dr. Luke, Jesus would have us to learn that our task is not to judge our neighbors but to love them. Our calling is not even to change them but simply to love them and to reveal Jesus to them. Jesus has the power to change people and will one day judge those who must be judged. In the meanwhile, his disciples are to show compassion to everyone.

The Parable of the Good Samaritan is unique to Luke. No other Gospel includes it. With a Samaritan rather than a Jew as its hero, the story points to the four kinds of people found in this world. First, there are victims such as the man who fell victim to robbers. Second, there are victimizers like the calloused thieves. Third, there are indifferent folk who are represented in the story by the priest and the Levite. Fourth, there are compassionate souls like the Samaritan.

Has anyone ever missed the point of this powerful story? The call is for God's people never to be either victimizers or indifferent souls. We may sometimes be victims. But we must make a conscious choice to be compassionate presences. Aware that our neighbors are not merely those most like us but anyone in need, Jesus calls us to love them.

This parable was told in response to the question "Who is my neighbor?" Jesus translated that question into "Whom shall we love?" and answered "Everyone!" Compassion is still something about which we have much to learn. Whoever is in your path and needs it becomes the proper object of your concern and aid. Stop debating the issue of who deserves your love, and go help somebody.

If the church would learn this lesson, the unbelieving world watching us would have its attention riveted on Jesus and be open to hearing his message.

The third thing is *personal faith*. There are people I know who have a hard time loving themselves. Accepting themselves. Believing that God loves and accepts them. There is something back there in the past. There is some doubt that won't go away, some vice that will not release you from its hold, or some sin that is utterly humiliating to you. The reasoning seems to go this way: Since I can't accept myself, therefore God cannot possibly accept me either. I've gone too far. I'm just too bad. It's hopeless.

The Gospel of Luke communicates the wonderful truth of divine grace. It affirms that God accepts people who are having a difficult time accepting themselves. That loving acceptance of sinners by their Creator-God is the ultimate implication of the truth that Jesus belongs to all of us.

Another parable from Jesus that is recorded only in Luke is the Parable of the Pharisee and the Tax Collector (18:9-14). No Stephen King thriller ever had a more unexpected ending than this story. Two men go up to the temple to pray. One is a respected churchman. All you have to do to know that is listen to his prayer. It is almost musical in its cadence. He is comfortable in prayer. He has a full command of prayer language and knows all the cliches about "sick and afflicted," "ready recollection," and so forth. Then there is another man praying that day. He is off in a dark corner. He doesn't even raise his head before God, and he may not have said his prayer aloud. In what may have been nothing more than a whisper, he prays, "God, have mercy on me, a sinner." In fact, the Greek text has him saying literally, "God, have mercy on me, *the* sinner." This man is serious about his sin. He sees himself as the only sinner in the world. No shifting of blame. No comparing his sins to someone else's sins (cf. 1 Tim. 1:15).

What was the story's surprise ending? Both men went home with what they wanted from worship that day. The Pharisee was seen and heard by men; he was confirmed in their sight as a man of piety. The tax collector was seen and heard by God; he went home forgiven. The sinner who was proud of his good works went home still sinful; the sinner who was broken and contrite about his sins went home justified. Anyone who comes to Jesus Christ with a heart broken by sin will not be turned away. His burden of guilt will be lifted lest he be crushed under it.

Conclusion

Luke presents a powerful picture of Jesus, and future chapters in this book will permit us to explore several of the most obvious ones. We will be seeing a Jewish Savior through Gentile eyes. We will be trying to catch Luke's "selling points" about Jesus in order to appreciate him more. As a result, we should be better prepared to share him with others. Perhaps we can even learn Luke's style of presenting Jesus with sensitivity to the life situations of people around us.

Luke wanted us to see Jesus with a full breadth of vision. He wanted us to see that Jesus can't be put in the tiny box of our expectations and traditions. He is not the possession of one proud race, a snobbish nation, or some exclusive denomination. He is God's gift to all of us.

For Reflection and Discussion

1. What is the distinctive quality of the Gospel of Matthew? Mark? John? What is the primary limitation of a harmony-of-the-Gospels approach to studying the Gospels?

2. In what sense are all four Gospels "faith-tracts"? How does this differ from seeing them as biographies?

3. What are some of the distinctive features of the Gospel of Luke?

4. Summarize what we can know of the man Luke from the New Testament. How did his background prepare him for the writing of this book?

5. Explain the thesis of *A Jewish Savior Through Gentile Eyes* that Luke focused on "selling points" about Jesus for the larger Roman world of his day.

6. Identify what the term *universalism* means as used in this chapter.

7. Review the texts cited as evidence that the theme of universalism was important to Luke. Can you identify others?

8. What are some of the connotations of universalism for our efforts at evangelism today? Are there nations, races, or classes of people who have been shunned in the church's evangelistic work?

9. Relate the Christian obligation of compassion to Luke's interest in universalism. Why is the Parable of the Good Samaritan such a challenging story?

10. How does personal faith relate to universalism in the Gospel of Luke? Do you know anyone struggling with the problem of self-acceptance?

Chapter 2

He Knows Your Name

Vladimir Souloukhin is a Soviet poet and essayist who has been a member of the Communist Party for over 30 years. A loyal party member. Well-known in the Soviet Union.

He wrote a piece in the Russian literary journal *Kommunist* a few years back that was really quite surprising. It preceded *glasnost* and *perestroika* by a decade. It was remarkably radical for its time.

His article insisted that "in the twentieth century, there is no doubt for every reasonable person that a supreme reason exists in the world, in the universe, in life." He closed with the affirmation that a denial of what he called a "supreme reason" would be to claim that such

> ... complicated and precise organisms as a flower, a bird, a human being and, finally, a human brain, appeared at random -- the result of a lucky, blind and unprogrammed combination of chemical elements. ...
>
> The question is not whether a supreme reason exists, but whether it knows about me and has anything to do with me.[1]

I quote Souloukhin from a Communist publication not only because it is so unlikely a source for a statement about "supreme reason" (he never used the word God in his essay) but also because of the way it closes. He said, "The question is not whether a supreme reason exists, *but whether it knows about me and has anything to do with me.*"

He raises the real challenge to Christian theism very effectively. Most simply stated, that challenge is the possi-

---

[1] Quoted in *Christianity Today*, Aug. 6, 1982, p. 13.

bility of a relationship with our Creator. I know God exists, but does he know that *I* exist? Does he *care* that I exist? *Does God know my name?*

Soloukhin is pointing to the critical issue for people of East and West. Everybody needs to be known. Everybody needs to be cared about. We like it when we find that someone is interested enough in us that he or she would even go to the trouble of learning and remembering our names.

Against the emphasis of *universalism* in the third Gospel (i.e., that Jesus Christ is the Savior of all), Luke is equally emphatic about *the importance of the individual* to God. The Son of Man saves all only because he knows each. He cares about us as unique beings.

For Luke, Christianity is not a mighty movement sweeping the masses before it. It is the personal love of God for people made in his image.

Luke tells us, for example, about many people we would otherwise never know. Over 50 percent of the material in the Gospel of Luke is unique to it.

Much of the unique material in Luke consists of personal sketches. Often it appears to be important for the physician-turned-evangelist to give the person's name rather than simply tell about "a certain man" or "a woman of Samaria." For example, concerning the birth of Christ, we wouldn't know the story of Zechariah and Elizabeth if Luke had not told it. The stories of Simeon and Anna recognizing the baby at the temple are told only in Luke. Luke was interested in the personal dimension.

If you move from the birth all the way to the end of Jesus' earthly ministry, there is a story of his walk along the Emmaeus Road. Luke is the only one who tells about that episode, and he names one of the two men Jesus met (i.e., Cleopas).

He tells certain personal stories in cameo-like style. The story about Mary and Martha is a perfect example

(10:38-42). Jesus was in their home, and Mary was sitting at his feet to hear him teach. Martha was worried because Mary was not helping in the kitchen. Luke is the only one who tells that story. The incident in the house of Simon the Pharisee (7:36-50) is another pearl unique to the third Gospel.

There is an ancient tradition which holds that Luke was a painter. Whether that is reliable or not, I cannot say. But he certainly saw events through an artist's eye and wrote of them with artistic clarity.

Luke is interested in the personal dimension. He notices people. He tells their personal, heartwarming, touching stories. Unlike Matthew, some writers have observed, Luke does not speak of Jesus' compassion on the multitude (cf. Matt. 9:36; 15:32) but focuses instead on his concern for individuals. This Gospel reminds us that no one is insignificant when seen through the eyes of God.

A Concept of Self

What does this emphasis in Luke teach us about how we should view ourselves?

You probably know the name Charlie Brown. He is the famous Charles Shultz cartoon character who sees himself as the world's biggest nothing. And Lucy is always ready to reinforce his self-image as a loser. "He's a real Charlie Brown" has become an American idiom for someone who is a klutz.

God never created a nobody! Every human being is of infinite worth because he or she bears the divine image. Each of us is loved beyond measure, and the best proof of that fact is Calvary.

Over the course of history, definitions of what it is to be human have arisen from many quarters.

There is the classical Greek view, the ancient view of Aristotle, which sees man as a *rational* being. Within this

23

frame of reference, reason is man's highest faculty. Mental processes are to dominate physical and emotional powers, and the ultimate goal of life is knowledge.

The physicalist view of both ancient and modern times is that man is a *mechanical* being. Man is complex but fully explainable by the natural sciences, and there is nothing ultimately unique to "human nature." A person such as B. F. Skinner sees man as a physical organism with a neural mechanism awaiting conditioning and programming. The self is merely the sum total of an individual's experiences, an integrated system of responses brought about by genetics and environment. The ultimate goal in life on a physicalist view is pleasure.

Then there is a view of humankind shared by Eastern religions and the New Age Movement which insists that man is *god*. It's a pantheistic system. Everything centers on self-awareness, self-fulfillment, and self-worship. It is an irrational system which fosters superstition and irresponsible behavior. The goal of life is generally thought of as peaceful absorption into the cosmos, a snuffing out of personal identity and selfhood altogether.

As an alternative to all these, there is the Christian view which goes beyond what any of the others can acknowledge. This view holds that males and females of the human race are *in God's image*. It acknowledges that man does have rational powers but insists that the final goal of life is not some sort of snobbish, mystical enlightenment. The Bible talks about the physical part of man and acknowledges the importance (even sacredness) of the body. But Scripture will have no part of the idea that man is in fact god, that man is both creator and creature to himself.

On the Christian view, man is in God's image. He is self-conscious, free, and morally responsible. Both males and females are of dignity and worth because God's likeness is stamped upon them (cf. Gen. 1:27). Mankind is capable of fellowship with God. In heart, soul, mind, and strength, the total person can be sanctified to God. Life can then be lived to God's glory through love and service to one's fellow human beings.

The Christian view of man is the highest and most complete view of what it is to be a creature on Planet Earth. *Man has dignity because he is more than just the apex of evolution. He has the stamp of God's own image on his very being.*

Luke's Concern for Individual Worth

Luke goes to great lengths to show how Jesus affirmed the worth of every human being, the dignity of every man and woman, which is something the first-century world didn't affirm. Whether pagan or Jewish, male or female, slave or free, God views us as beings of equal worth before him.

For example, the parables unique to Luke tend to focus on persons and their worth. There are 34 parables in Luke.[2] Of those parables, 18 are unique to Luke: The Two Debtors (7:41-43), The Good Samaritan (10:30-37), The Friend at Midnight (11:5-10), The Rich Fool (12:13-21), The Watching Servants (12:35-40), The Faithful Steward (12:42-48), The Barren Fig Tree (13:6-9), The Chief Seats (14:7-11), The Great Supper (14:16-24), The Unfinished Tower (14:28-30), The Unwaged War (14:31-33), The Lost Coin (15:8-10), The Lost Boy (15:11-32), The Shrewd Manager (16:1-15), The Unprofitable Servant (17:7-10), The Persistent Widow (18:1-8), The Pharisee and the Publican (18:9-14), and The Ten Minas (19:11-27). It is not difficult to see how these unique-to-Luke stories affirm personhood and personal worth.

[2] Note: Some would count 35 parables by including The Rich Man and Lazarus story among the parables. I take the story to be historical narrative because it is neither called a parable nor does it have some of the characteristic features of a parable.

For example, take the story of The Two Debtors. One man owes 500 denari, and the other owes 50. Both have their debts cancelled. Which will love more? Well, the one forgiven the greater debt. Jesus said, "That's correct. You've answered properly." Do you remember the setting for this story? Jesus was in the home of Simon the Pharisee, and a "sinful woman" had washed Jesus' feet with tears, dried them with her hair, and poured perfume on them.

Jesus turned to Simon and said, "Do you see this woman? I came into your house. You did not give me any water for my feet, but she wet them with her tears and wiped them with her hair. You did not give me a kiss, but this woman since the time I entered has not stopped kissing my feet. You did not put oil on my head, but she has poured perfume on my feet. Therefore, I tell you, her sins have been forgiven -- for she loved much."

Why do you think Luke would tell a story like that? Because it contrasts the attitude of Simon toward that sinful woman with his own toward her. Jesus would not reject or turn away from anybody who came to him. A woman. A prostitute. Jesus would not mistreat her. When she began to weep, wipe his feet with her hair, and perfume them, Jesus was probably as embarrassed as you would have been. But he would not flinch and pull back and embarrass her. Jesus said, "Simon, learn something from this woman. She is a sinner, but she admits it. And her many sins are forgiven because God loves her just as he loves you."

Very different, isn't it, from the way that we some-times treat people who put us in embarrassing spots? I find it interesting that, when Jesus tells parables, he tells them in situations like this to affirm people. To defend them. To tell us that we are to reach out to the people we find it hardest to accept.

The Parable of the Good Samaritan is also unique to Luke. In the familiar story, the Samaritan traveler looks at a man who had been beaten and robbed. With peril for himself, he went and administered to him. This seems to me to be a story that affirms an interest in persons.

Some of these parables that deal with personal worth are among the best-known and best-loved stories of all time. There is no more beautiful story in all literature than The Parable of the Lost Boy (or Prodigal Son).

The miracles that are unique to Luke also focus on personhood and the affirmation of individuals. They focus on people. There are 20 miracles in Luke, with seven of them unique to this Gospel: a miraculous catch of fish (5:1-11), raising a widow's son (7:11-17), casting out a demon (11:14), healing a crippled woman (13:10-17), healing a man with dropsy (14:1-4), healing ten lepers (17:11-19), and restoring Malchus' ear (22:49-51). These seven miracles have to do with affirming personal worth.

For example, in Luke 13:10, there is the account of a woman who had been crippled for 18 years. She came to Jesus one day, bent and stooped. The text indicates that her crippling was related to demon possession. At any rate, she "could not straighten up at all." When Jesus saw the woman in her pitiful condition, he called her to himself, touched her, and set her free from her infirmity. But some Pharisees who witnessed it criticized it because the healing had taken place on the Sabbath.

Do you remember how Jesus answered and defended himself? He said, "Doesn't each of you on the Sabbath untie his ox or donkey from the stall and lead it out to give it water?" He continued, "Then should not this woman . . . be set free on the Sabbath day from what bound her?" You see, rules meant more to those critics than people. Jesus taught that day that people are worth more than rules and that rules are meant to bless people rather than burden them.

At the end of the Gospel, there is a story which winds up being an account of a miracle. Soldiers were coming out to get Jesus on the night of his betrayal. After Judas identified him for the mob, something of a scuffle broke out. Peter jumped in and pulled out his knife and took a swipe at one of the mob members within his reach. The man was Malchus, and Peter's wild swing hit a glancing blow on the side of his head and severed his ear.

Look at this situation closely. This man is an enemy come to do Jesus harm. He is one of the most aggressive ones there. He is at the front of the group. Jesus, in the midst of the jeopardy in which he found himself, reached over and touched the man. He healed his ear by a miracle.

Stories such as these show the worth of people for both Jesus and Luke. Why do you think Luke would tell so many stories of this sort about Jesus? He wanted to let us know that Jesus didn't see masses. Didn't love groups. Didn't value only big crowds. Jesus loved every single person he encountered.

Going beyond the parables and the miracles, think next about Luke's choice of ministry encounters from Jesus' career. I call them "ministry encounters," for they are just conversations, questions, challenges, or exchanges. Every Gospel records several of these, but the following eight are unique to Luke: rejection at Nazareth (4:15-30), the anointing at Simon's house (7:36-50), the Seventy (10:1-12, 17-24), with Mary and Martha (10:38-42), Zacchaeus (19:1-10), women of Jerusalem (23:27-31), the penitent thief (23:39-43), and the Emmaeus Road encounter (24:13-35).

Let me just remind you of the particulars of only two of these. Jesus entered Jericho once, and the streets were lined with people. There was one eager fellow who could not see Jesus because he was so short. So he climbed up a tree. Jesus stopped, had a conversation with him, and ended by saying he would like to go to his house and talk further. It is the story of Jesus and Zacchaeus. Luke is the only one who tells it. Luke could not overlook the fact that Jesus, surrounded by a mob, would stop to pick out a single receptive person in the group (though probably the most unlikely in the eyes of everyone there!) with whom to share the good news of salvation.

Maybe an even more unlikely personal encounter was when Jesus took an interest in an individual at Luke 23:39. Jesus was dying on the cross. The two thieves on either side had been saying horrible things about him. Do you realize that it is only Luke who tells us that one of those thieves later thought better of what he was doing and repented? He said, "Jesus, remember me when you come in your kingdom." And Jesus answered him, "I tell you the truth, today you will be with me in paradise." He was dying for the sins of the whole world, but even then he would not miss the chance to save one penitent thief who had been hurling reproach at him for the whole day up to that point.

God's "Tender Mercy"

In his wonderful Gospel, Luke develops the doctrine of God's "tender mercy" for his people.

There is an unusual term used by him in 1:78. It occurs in Zechariah's song that was composed to Jesus. He used the word for "entrails" or "bowels." It was commonly used by Greek writers to denote anger.

The word in question is *splagchna*. Quite literally, it refers to one's inner parts or bowels. It made its way into Greek vocabulary to signify the inner emotions one might feel and associate with the churning of his stomach or with some other physical sensation.

As used by Christians, though, the word came to signify warmth and compassion. Inner-mercy feelings. Thus, tender mercy. As Luke used the term, with his medical training perhaps playing word-games in his head, it is not difficult to imagine his choice of the word.

So, beginning at 1:78, Luke develops this doctrine of the *tender mercies of God*. He affirms that God's compassion reaches out to every one of his creatures. He pictures God's passions aroused for the sake of humanity. This doctrine which affirms God's care for us is developed on every page of the third Gospel. It is a bold and striking term to use when speaking of God. It demands that we visualize a God who cares for us.

In Luke 12:1-7, watch the writer's artistry in painting a word picture of God. He tells of Jesus talking about sparrows. Why, they are practically worthless. You could buy five of them for a couple of small coins. But, claimed Jesus, God doesn't lose sight of even one of those sparrows. What is his point? If God pays attention to the smallest and most insignificant parts of his creation, he will not forget men and women he made in his image. "Don't be afraid," he said, "you are worth more than many sparrows."

God's care for us is so great that "the very hairs of your head are all numbered," a much easier job with some of us than with others. It is hyperbole designed to emphasize God's personal concern.

The God we serve is not a God of mass movements. And Christianity is not a religion that seeks to start something rolling in the hope that somehow the band wagon will gain enough momentum so that all races and peoples and tribes will jump on.

Our God loves people for their individual worth and personhood. God affirms their dignity, so it is all right for them to accept the fact that they have worth before him.

Conclusion

I read a book a few years ago titled *The Jesus Style*. I have come to treasure it. I think so much of it that I have recommended it to dozens of people and bought gift copies for several. There are markings all over the pages of my copy. Corners of some pages have been turned down so some especially significant lines can be found quickly.

The book impressed me so much that I wanted to communicate with the man who wrote it to thank him for his work. I'd never done that over a book before.

Against the sort of natural reluctance one feels in approaching someone with whom he has had no previous contact, I risked getting the phone number of Gayle Erwin. What happened then was not what I expected.

"Mr. Erwin? This is Rubel Shelly in Nashville, Tennessee," I began. "I wanted to call you and . . . "

"Oh yes," he interrupted. "I remember you. I came to hear you speak earlier this year. I hope you don't mind, but I've been quoting something you said in a speech I have made at a few places out here on the Coast."

What? He knew *my* name? This fellow who had written a book that had helped me? A man who had written a book which was the Selection of the Month for the two largest religious book clubs in the United States had heard me speak?

Isn't that a small-scale episode of what Luke is trying to tell us in his Gospel?

I think I understand why a Greek physician would make a major point of this personal concern of God to the Gentile world of his time. Their religions didn't have much personal dimension to them then. And many people are still asking the same question Vladimir Soloukhin asked. Is God aware of me? Does he concern himself with my situation?

Luke said that the God who showed himself to us in the person of Jesus Christ is a God who attaches great worth to every creature in his image and wants everyone saved without the loss of one.

He knows your name. He cares about you. He knows where you hurt. He knows you have sinned. He knows all that about you, but he comes to you personally. Not in some abstract manner. Not by issuing an invitation

31

to the masses. But by calling your name and asking that you let him save you.

He knows *your* name.

For Reflection and Discussion

1. Put the issue of Soloukhin's statement in your own words. Why is this such a critical matter?

2. Do you see a possible tension between the themes of *universalism* and *the importance of each individual*? How does Luke resolve the tension?

3. Recount some of the unique stories in the Gospel of Luke that point to Luke's concern for individuals. Have you ever known of a person or group losing sight of the individual for the sake of a mass movement?

4. Trace the three competing theories of human nature identified in this chapter. What does each imply about the worth and meaning of a single human life?

5. State the distinctive Judeo-Christian view of human life revealed in Scripture. What does it imply about the worth and meaning of a single human life?

6. Show how the parables unique to Luke affirm personhood and personal worth. Reflect on one which is not discussed in the text of this book and show how it fits the pattern.

7. Show how the miracles unique to Luke affirm personhood and personal worth. Again, choose one that is not discussed in this volume.

8. Do the same exercise as in questions 7 and 8 with one of the "ministry encounters" unique to Luke.

9. Interpret the doctrine of the "tender mercies of God" from the Gospel of Luke. What does it say about you as seen through God's eyes?

10. What is the greatest single obstacle to your ability to believe that God knows your name and cares about you as an individual?

Chapter 3

From Property to Partnership

Ancient cultures accorded very little respect to women. In his own day and time, Jesus affirmed the dignity of females. He broke the rules of his culture and challenged the myth of female inferiority. His attitude toward women and his willingness to allow them to be numbered among his disciples set him apart from other rabbis of his time.

No, the claim is not that Jesus would adopt the full agenda of today's radical feminists. But there can be no doubt that an element of his ministry was devoted to the affirmation of the dignity and worth of women.

Women were often regarded as property in antiquity. A woman was a father's to barter; he would get the best price he could for himself in arranging her marriage. After her wedding, that woman was her husband's property to use or abuse as he chose. Some cultures would not even bring legal charges against a man if he put his wife to death. She was counted as the man's property, thus she didn't have the rights of a human being.

Women typically had about the same rights as a slave. In legal texts from ancient cultures, women and slaves are mentioned in the same provision. A slave had no rights under law, and, as a rule, neither did a woman.

Women were generally regarded as sexual devices. Playthings to men. Childbearers to those who were married. Women seldom appeared in public except to draw water, perhaps to herd animals, or to do other work that might require her to venture out of the house.

They were offered very little education. In some cultures it was considered seditious to teach a woman to read. The danger was, of course, that education might undermine the right of men to take advantage of them in a male-dominated society.

Women in Hebrew Culture

Things weren't a lot better within Jewish culture. The Old Testament itself, both in narrative and in law, presents women in a much more positive light than most ancient documents. She is a "helper suited to man" who is bone of his bones and flesh of his flesh (Gen. 2:18, 23). She has a relationship with man that is unique. While her primary duties were pictured as domestic ones, she was nevertheless to be honored for doing them. That is, she was not to be viewed simply as a dutiful slave.

In Lemuel's poem about the "wife of noble character" at Proverbs 31, many of her duties are carried out in the home. Yet she does several things which involve public visibility and a significant degree of personal independence. She "considers a field and buys it," administers the duties of servants under her, and trades items she has manufactured with merchants. Much of her husband's stature in the community appears to be tied to her image and performance. Her children respect her and "call her blessed," and her husband "praises her."

Although it does not sound radical to us, the Ten Commandments go well beyond most ancient codes of law in requiring that children honor both their fathers and their mothers (Ex. 20:12; cf. Lev. 19:3). In the absence of male heirs, a woman under Jewish law could even inherit property and be a landowner. That, too, was unusual in ancient literature (Num. 17:1-11).

Although the Law afforded considerable respect to females, a woman's social position in Jewish culture at the time of Christ reflected many male prejudices.

In worship, for example, they were more often observers than participants. The synagogue segregated women from men and kept them out of view. Rabbinic discussions of women were very sexist and chauvinistic. Women were regarded as temptresses and seductresses. "Thus, under no circumstances should a man walk behind a woman, not even his own wife. One who walks behind a woman crossing a stream has no share in the World to Come."[1]

Jewish women could not testify in court except under the rarest of circumstances. Even in these rare situations, according to the Talmud, "Women, even a hundred of them, are legally equal to one male witness."[2] So two dozen women might testify to a matter, but, if a man's word contradicted them, the man's word would likely carry the day.

Although a husband could divorce his wife by simply giving her a certificate of divorce, women could not divorce their husbands.

Women were excluded from those eligible to lay hands on an animal to be offered in sacrifice. Along with minors, the mentally deranged, slaves, and Gentiles, this privilege did not belong to them.

One of the Eighteen Benedictions used in synagogue worship went: "I thank you, Lord, that I was not born a Gentile, a slave, or a woman." The woman's version of the same prayer went: "I thank you, Lord, that you have made me according to your will." So, even when it is granted that what the Old Testament says was appropriate to give a woman some degree of dignity and protection under law, Jewish culture was typically just as sexist and chauvinistic as pagan culture.

Rabbis did not include women as their disciples. Some regarded it as a sin to teach women. Rabbi Eliezer said, "If any man gives his daughter a knowledge of the Law

---

[1] George Foot Moore, *Judaism in the First Centuries of the Christian Era*, Vol. II (New York: Schocken Books), p. 269.

[2] *Yebamoth* 115a.

it is as though he taught her lechery."[3] If you saw the Barbra Streisand movie *Yentl*, you will recall her character's frustration at the opening of the film about being denied the study of the Law. That reflects the classic attitude of the disdain in traditional Judaism for a woman being allowed to be a disciple, a learner, a student of the Torah. Among the stricter rabbis, there was a tradition of never speaking to a woman in public, not even to one's own mother, wife, or daughter.

The Christian attitude toward women was radical for the time and was one of Luke's "selling points" in presenting a Jewish Savior to the larger world. Jesus had no power to change law or culture. His behavior, example, and teaching, though, set a revolutionary new precedent for a woman's self-esteem and for the Christian treatment of women.

Women in the Gospel of Luke

As a Gentile, Luke knew the disregard for women in his culture. What his own initial reaction to Jesus on this point was, we can only guess. But it seems to have made a very positive impression on him.

Vincent Taylor says that Luke mentions 13 women not referred to in the other Gospels.

In connection with the birth and infancy of Jesus, Luke tells of Elizabeth, the mother of John and cousin of Mary, and her interaction with Mary the mother of Jesus (1:5-25).

Luke also tells of a detailed event that centers on Mary. It's a lovely portrait of a very gentle and godly young woman. In the genealogy of Jesus that is given in Luke, which is different than the one in Matthew, he traces the genealogy through Mary. Matthew, as a typical Jew, is concerned to trace his legal genealogy through Joseph his

---

[3] Mishnah, *Sotah* 3:4.

foster father.

In Luke's account of the life of Jesus, he pointed to a number of distinctives. At least eight of these can be identified, and there may be others you can find.

First, consider the fact that Jesus treated women with respect and dignity, unlike the rabbis. In Luke 7:44-48, while a sinful woman at the house of Simon the Pharisee was weeping at the feet of Jesus, Simon (with typical Jewish disdain) wondered why Jesus would allow it. Jesus explained by pointing to two things about her. First, he observed the woman's obvious love for God as proved by her behavior toward Jesus. Second, he forgave her sins.

Simon treated her according to the typical expectations of his time. Jesus treated her very differently. He affirmed her, forgave her, and accepted her.

Second, Jesus worked miracles for the benefit of women. In Luke 8:40-56, there is an interesting interweaving of two stories. A man named Jairus came to Jesus. He had a little daughter who was only 12, and she was dying. Do you know what a 12-year-old girl was worth in ancient cultures? Do you know what the death of a girl was considered in relation to the death of a boy? Boys were worth something. They were economically valuable. But Luke tells the story of a man who was concerned about his little girl.

Jesus was concerned enough about Jairus' daughter that he was willing to go with the man to his house. By the time they got there, she was dead. Even then Jesus didn't dismiss the matter. He took Peter, James, and John inside, and he raised her back to life.

Interestingly, from the time Jairus met Jesus and asked him to come until their arrival, the traveling group passed by another woman who came up to Jesus. She had been hemorrhaging for years. Now there's a footnote in some of the manuscripts of this Gospel that gives a tidbit which sounds very much like our author. It says the woman had suffered this condition for 12 years "and she had spent all she had on doctors." The reason for saying this note sounds like Luke is probably obvious to you. He was a physician, remember? So that fact about her registered. Here's a woman that he couldn't have helped. She touched Jesus in faith seeking to be healed, however, and she was made whole. When Jesus asked, "Who touched me?", the woman identified herself. Instead of rebuking her, Jesus said, "Daughter, your faith has healed you. Go in peace."

Third, he taught women. When Mary sat with him to listen to him teach, he did not shoo her away, not even when Martha asked that she be sent to the kitchen to help her prepare dinner (10:38-42; cf. John 4:27).

Fourth, he included women among his disciples, and they were among his most faithful followers. Mary Magdalene, Joanna, Susanna, and some other women provided financial support for Jesus and his apostles (8:1-3). Women were part of the traveling band of disciples who occasionally went with Jesus throughout Galilee, Samaria, and Judea (23:49).

Fifth, he was compassionate with women. Thus the healing of a crippled woman who had been bound by a spirit for 18 years (13:10-17). In the account of healing this poor woman, Jesus affectionately referred to her "a daughter of Abraham" (v. 10).

Sixth, he used the actions of a woman as an example to all others. Upon seeing a poor woman put two small copper coins into the temple treasury, Jesus praised her gift as greater than anyone else's that day and held her sacrificial spirit to be worthy of imitation (21:1-4).

Seventh, he even stopped to teach a group of women as he was making his anguished way to Golgotha (23:27-31).

Eighth, women were witnesses of his resurrection (23:55 - 24:11). In fact, women were the first witnesses of this event and the first to bear witness of it to others (cf.

John 20:11-18).

We Still Have Much to Learn

We still have a lot to learn from Jesus on this subject. Culture and tradition have overshadowed Jesus' example and teaching. Even though our secular culture speaks feminist rhetoric, it nonetheless continues to degrade women. Often it does so with their complicity.

In modern Western culture, women are frequently nothing more than sex objects in many entertainment settings. They are mindless bodies on display for ogling, catcalls, teasing, and gaping.

A report about sexually violent movies and what they do to affect the way men think about women was published a while back in *Psychology Today*. Some men in a series of tests were shown X-rated films over a period of time, and then they were shown a re-enactment of a rape trial. According to the study, "The victim of rape rated as significantly more worthless and her injury as significantly less severe by those men who had been exposed to filmed violence than by a control group who saw only the rape trial and did not view any of our films." Yet the libertarians in our midst insist that we must protect pornographers' rights to produce and exhibit this sort of "entertainment."

The way women are often presented in films (i.e., as objects of violence and rape) creates a calloused attitude. And there is still the myth that circulates among some males that women want to be treated with some degree of violence and force against their persons.

The reason Gary Hart lost in his bid for the Democratic presidential nomination for the 1988 campaign was not an "error in judgment." He lost because he thought men could champion the causes of women and then still treat them as sexual playthings, as something less than human beings.

The abuse of women in domestic settings is something that our society is not yet dealing with very well. What some call "the silent crime" is only beginning to get the attention it deserves. Six million wives will be abused by their husbands this year. Close to 4,000 will be beaten to death. Battery is the single most frequent cause of injury to women, outpacing by far such things as rapes, muggings, or even auto accidents.

Women are harassed in the public workplace. Typically they are not paid a wage equal to that of men who are doing the same work. Women will be jerked around and treated as men would not be treated when a company moves from one place to another or when job changes are underfoot.

Then there is the sexual harassment that women are subjected to in the marketplace. It may be as subtle as a leer or as direct as a pinch. A national newsmagazine carried an article on this phenomenon which told of a typist in New York whose boss offered her a raise if she would sleep with him, of a freshman university student whose instructor tried to kiss her when she went to his office, of a secretary who quit her job after her boss and three other men watched her lock a long row of filing cabinets and then called out, "Isn't she a cutie?" Do you really think Jesus would be party to such things or silent in the face of them?

Then there is the depreciation of the traditional role of woman as wife and mother in our culture as a nonproductive career. That attitude encourages women who choose that role in our culture to see their work as somehow not significant enough to give them worth and self-esteem. Some women think they need to abandon marriage and motherhood in order to find fulfillment.

The Christian tradition is open to criticism in this area as well as the culture generally. You want to guess who said this? "Woman is a necessary evil, a national tempta-tion, a desirable calamity, a domestic peril, a deadly fascination, and a painful ill." The quote is from John Chrysostom, a fourth-century preacher. Or try to guess the source of this: "If a woman becomes weary, or at last dead from childbearing, that matters not; she is there to do it." That's from no less than Martin Luther.

I attended a lecture given by a well-known Christian leader of our time. The lecturer's theme was marriage and the family. Here was his counsel to women who were being physically abused: "I don't care if your husband is mean and as tough as nails. You must submit to him. It is the will of God." Jesus taught no such low view of any human being, whether male or female.

Some "traditionalists" have equated male headship with dominance and female submission with inferiority. Women are not saved through men. They are saved directly by Jesus Christ (Gal. 3:26-28). A woman is responsible to God for her own salvation and spiritual growth in Christ (1 Pet. 3:7). Her submission to her husband or to the male leadership of the church does not denigrate her before God. Christ's submission is her model, and the submission he gave to his father did not degrade him and did not affirm his inferiority. A relationship of headship for males in families and church is ordained of God. But what is not ordained of God are the leaps beyond that which we have taken in our culture and tradition to demean women.

In brief summary, Scripture teaches that the sexes are equal in bearing the *Imago Dei* and in their standing before God. Yet males are to exercise leadership authority both in the home and in the church. As Christ is the head of his church, so the husband is the head of his wife (1 Cor. 11:3); in the spiritual family of God which is his church, it is prohibited for "a woman to teach or to have authority over a man" (1 Tim. 2:12). However, in exercising their leadership, men are to follow Christ's example of humility (Phil. 2:3-5) and mutual service (Eph. 4:12). In the

41

words of Bruce Waltke: "The Christian symbol of hierarchy is not the scepter but the cross. This model of government stands in stark contrast to that of the world, where men and women seek self-fulfillment and want to dominate. The Bible offers a better alternative."

The goal and function of responsible male leadership is to open creative avenues for service and meaningful responsibility for women both in family and church settings. To use the role of headship as an excuse to belittle or to mistreat women is sinful.

Conclusion

One of the issues our generation is concerned about is respect for women.

As Luke did in his Gospel, we must present Jesus as the champion of female dignity rather than its enemy. Our failure to do so, coupled with our failure to exhibit his attitude in the life of the church, has functioned negatively to keep sensitive people from Christ. We must teach and practice the things Jesus did in all areas, including the dignity of women. The church must be bold enough to *say* what he said and even bolder to *do* what he did.

In this culture, it must be a primary point of emphasis that women under God have the dignity, worth, and respect that Jesus showed them in his own life and ministry. If we fail to affirm what Luke did, we will not be faithful to Christ as he was.

For Reflection and Discussion

1. What was the typical status of women in ancient pagan cultures? Why were they often listed with slaves in ancient civil codes?

2. In what specific ways was the Old Testament different from most ancient law codes concerning the rights and dignity of women?

3. Did Old Testament laws result in a more elevated social status for women in Jewish culture? What was their status in Jewish society?

4. How radical was Jesus' treatment of women in light of his historical context?

5. Review the eight distinctive features of Jesus' treatment of women in the Gospel of Luke. What is the cumulative effect of these facts on you?

6. Identify some of the ways women are degraded in literature, movies, and TV today. Can you cite a current specific example?

7. How does our society (e.g., workplace) treat women in today's world? Are things getting better or worse, in your opinion?

8. What do you know about domestic violence in this country? How widespread is the problem?

9. Modern feminism has often appeared to depreciate the traditional role of women as wife and mother as a "nonproductive career." Can you give an instance of this sort of intimidation of women?

10. How has religion aided and abetted some of these mistreatments of women? What are some specific questions in this regard that must be addressed by the church today?

Chapter 4

Jesus Loves the Little Children

All three synoptic Gospels show Jesus interacting with and showing concern for children. While Luke is not alone in calling attention to this feature of the Savior's life (cf. Matt. 19:13-15; Mark 10:13-16), he seems to have had a more extensive interest in this phenomenon than any other Spirit-guided writer and often gives details the others omit.

Children have historically been given little protection in society. For example, we know several ancient cultures which placed such a premium on strength and skill in combat that imperfect children were regarded as expendable. Consider the ancient city-state of Sparta.

Will Durant, in his multi-volume *The Story of Civilization*, devoted a volume to life in ancient Greece. He wrote about Sparta's customs regarding children. When a child was born, the infant was carried to the father. The father would acknowledge or disown the child as his own. If the child was a girl, he might not accept her. If the child was deformed physically or somehow seemed not robust and healthy enough to achieve the warrior-ideal, the father could make the decision that the baby was to be discarded. There would be no one to question his decision.

If the father decided to accept the child, there was a state board appointed to examine children. The newborn would then be carried to the board. Its members would examine the child. If it did not look healthy, if the child had a bad foot, had a deformed hand, had any sort of birthmark that would in any way appear to compromise the child for the warrior-ideal of the city, the committee would give orders to a servant who, without further consultation with the family, would take the child up to Mt. Taygetus to throw it over a cliff.

Law and public opinion at Athens fostered similar practices. Any father had the right to expose a child to death that was doubted to be his own, physically weak, or deformed. The abandoned child would be left in a large earthenware jar in a public place. If anyone wished to rescue the child and adopt him or her, that was permitted. Otherwise, sanitation workers would dispose of the jar and its contents.

Plato, highly regarded for his ethical philosophy on many points, recommended that children of "inferior" persons and "any of the other sort who are born defective" should be disposed of by the guardians of the state.[1]

Our Sorry Track Record With Children

Lest we begin to feel smug that we are fortunate to live so far this side of atrocities like that against children, that we are far removed from a time in history when children were given no respect or protection, perhaps we should pause to reflect on the attitudes and actions of our own generation. There is a good possibility that we not only have not advanced too far, but that we have even made some of these crimes against children more feasible on a grand scale.

The sorriness of our modern track record with children can be traced in terms of three issues: abortion, abuse, and absence.

What about *abortion* in America? In 1973 the infamous *Roe v. Wade* decision was made. Somewhere between 18 and 20 million babies have been aborted legally in this country since that time. Something over one and a half million abortions are being performed every year. That means something over 4,000 each day, 365 days a year.

While granting that a woman has the right to control her own body, I deny that a fetus with a genetic code distinct

[1]*Republic* 460C.

46

from that woman's, perhaps even of a different sex and blood type from her, is "her own body." There is another body growing within her womb, and that body has some rights of her/his own. Something has to be wrong with the ethical wisdom that holds the destruction of a bald eagle's unhatched egg to be a criminal act punishable by a year in prison and a $100,000 fine but allows the destruction of a human being *in utero* to be construed as a purely private matter which should not be subject to legal restraint.

What about child *abuse*? Many people hide their eyes from the reality of child abuse in this "enlightened and civilized society" of ours. I happened to be in Portland, Oregon, when a story broke there about this problem. The front page of the newspaper carried a story titled "Children flogged, officials say."[2] The article told of 55 children who apparently had been housed in a religious commune on the outskirts of Portland in a four-bedroom house with one toilet, no food, and no beds. Some children had been beaten with as many as 800 blows while all the other children were forced to watch the beatings and count the blows.

This horrible case came to the attention of authorities because one child didn't survive her beating. An eight-year-old girl was pronounced dead on arrival at an emergency room. An investigation followed, and the story was carried across the country.

Something around two million child abuse cases have been reported in the United States each year for the past several years. That is up from 413,000 cases in 1976 and 851,000 in 1981. Will the 1990s be better?

Then what are we to make of America's *absence* from her children? What does the term "absence" signify in relation to children? Let me explain.

One out of five children today in the United States of America lives in a single-parent home (i.e., a home where at

[2]*Oregonian*, Oct. 18, 1988, p. 1.

least one parent is absent). I realize that not all these situations can be avoided. Some of them are single-parent families because of death. Others are single-parent families because a marriage failed and could not be salvaged.

But a lot of homes are single-parent homes because selfish adults got so caught up in their rights, their pains, their freedoms, their desires, and their wants that they are willfully absent. To take themselves from their children. To walk away from the responsibilities they accepted when they brought children into the world. Sociologists say that three of every five children born in 1990 will live in a single-parent home at some point in his or her development before reaching age 18.

Simple human dignity and the Golden Rule are overrun when children, with their unrestrained love and unquestioning trust, are betrayed by society. It is instructive to see Luke call attention to little children and to the fact that Jesus loved them so.

Children in the Gospel of Luke

The Gospel of Luke opens with the story of a childless couple, Zechariah and Elizabeth. Luke documents their grief over having no children (1:7, 18, 25). Then he writes of their joy over the birth of the child John, a baby they received as a gift from God. Some interesting statements about their child are found at 1:15, 66, and 80.

Then there is greater focus on the birth and boyhood of Jesus in Luke than in any other Gospel. The narrative opens with the angel's announcement to Mary (1:26-38). The events of the birth at Bethlehem are recorded (2:1-7). There is the circumcision of Jesus on the eighth day in Bethlehem (2:21). Then his presentation at the temple in Jerusalem 40 days after his birth (2:22-24). The reactions of Simeon and Anna (2:25-38). These details are unparalleled in Matthew, Mark, and John. It is as if Luke wanted us to understand that the whole of a human life is important, that children as well as adults matter to God.

In this Gospel, a wide array of Jesus' interactions with children is chronicled. Luke tells how he healed the widow of Nain's son (7:11-15, cf. v. 12). Brought back to life the daughter of Jairus (8:41-56, cf. v. 42). Healed a boy who had been tormented by a demon that caused him to thrash about, roll into fires, and be burned (9: 38-43, cf. v. 38).

A fascinating thing about these three accounts is that Luke used a word when referring to each of the children involved which signifies how precious they were to their parents. The Greek word is *monogenes.* Dearly loved. Irreplaceable to that parent's heart. Incomparable in their sight. It's the same word used in John 3:16 of Jesus in relation to the Father in heaven.

Luke saw the compassion that parents could have for children, and he went to great lengths to talk about it. For example, he tells of situations like the one in chapter 18 where Jesus used children to emphasize the virtues of remaining teachable, trusting God, loving people, and being humble.

In Luke 7:32, there is an episode where Jesus quotes a song or a limerick that the children used in their games. That he knew it suggests that children were often around when Jesus taught. He was warm and affectionate with them. Why, his very presence must have attracted them to him. And it is not difficult at all to believe that he would relax from some of his full days of teaching and activity by playing with the children. Can't you just see him on his knees, hugging them? Playing with them? Singing the song whose lines he quoted with them?

Both children and adults matter to God. Jesus proved it by his behavior with them.

A Conspiracy Against Childhood

Though Jesus was warm and accepting with children, I sometimes get the feeling that we have entered a conspiracy against children. Against childhood itself.

Life used to have a period of innocence built in on the front end that some of us are taking away from our children. It was a time when children could just be children. They didn't have to go to pre-pre-pre-kindergarten in order to do well in pre-pre-kindergarten so they could be reading by age three and doing long division before they got into first grade!

Here's a case study. A mother is in the park playing with her baby. Holding the baby up. Blowing on his tummy and making him laugh. Talking baby talk. Another mother on a bench leans over and says, "You know it's a serious mistake to make those nonsense baby-talk sounds. It interferes with good patterns of speech development." Relax with your children and let them revel in being children. Are we taking away innocence? Rushing our children? Over-organizing their lives? Putting them under stress?

One specialist in childhood education summed it up this way: "We seem more and more determined to get children who will 'produce' and 'conform.' We really like children best when they stop being children and become adults."

An interesting study shows that children who are taught to read in those pre-pre-kindergarten classes at age four read no better by the fourth grade than their classmates whose first instruction in reading was given in first grade.

We sometimes appear to have the idea that our children need to live lives as stressed out as the ones we're living as adults. So, every child has to be in ballet, has to be in scouting, has to be in karate, has to be in little league, has to be in soccer. Don't get me wrong. I'm not putting down these things for kids. For kids who want them, enjoy them, and seek them, let them have a go at them. Make friends. Learn skills.

But I've seen children so programmed by their parents that they didn't have time to be children. They had to get to their next appointment and their next lesson. I've seen mothers cross and irritable because they have had to make all those schedules. They had to get them to practice, and dads had to show up for all the performances. It's been destructive to the family. They'd have been much better off going to a public park for unstructured play on the swings one afternoon a week.

Do we want a world of performing intellectual seals who all read at age two? Conditioned-response training of preschoolers who satisfy some set of artificial standards? Or wouldn't it be better to produce people who have been given the right to experience all of life's developmental stages, including childhood?

Consider the case of a boy studying the Ten Commandments who was asked to use the word *covet* in a sentence: "I go to school five days a week. I take piano and karate lessons. I go to scout meetings and church youth group activities. How I would *covet* a day to goof off and do nothing!"

What's wrong with children just being children? Playing in the yard with mom and dad? Playing in the sprinkler in the warm times of the year? What's wrong with children being children? This conspiracy against childhood needs to end.

Perhaps you followed the story of Adragon De Mello in the national press. He was one of those precocious children who could read and write at age two. At five he was a member of Mensa, an elite group that allows the upper two percent of people in IQ percentiles across the country to have membership. At eight, he enrolled in a community college in Santa Cruz, California. At age 11, he graduated from the University of California with a bachelor's degree in mathematics. According to the *1989 Guinness Book of World Records*, Adragon De Mello was the world's youngest college graduate.

In October 1988, however, the child was taken away from his father. The father was charged with inflicting "unjustifiable physical pain and/or mental suffering" on the boy. As the story was told in the *New York Times*, Adragon was a child with average intelligence. His father had been doing part of his homework and had been hiring other parts of it done. Teachers first became suspicious when the young student couldn't do in class what he could bring in on homework papers. At first some offered the explanation that his problem was the stress of performing in front of others. As time went on, however, the truth came out.

The boy's father apparently determined that Adragon would be a "trained intellectual seal" to perform on signal. So the boy's life was lived by an agenda set by the father. That agenda was not in the boy's best interest but was for his father's purposes. He apparently was getting some sort of vicarious delight out of seeing the child given accolades.

Yes, it is an extreme case. A bizarre case. But other versions of the same thing happen too often. And, while "pushy parents" are not all equivalent to Adragon De Mello's father, they would be better advised to allow their children to develop naturally. Encourage and inspire your children. But don't make them live your agenda or fulfill your dreams.

Responsibilities to Our Children

All of us owe some things to the children who have been brought into this world. Who has the responsibility for them? What are our obligations?

First, society has a responsibility to the children in it. In a word, *society must protect its children.*

The responsibility of a society to protect its children certainly involves listening to the screams of children who are being abused. When the world's heart was broken over the death of little six-year-old Lisa Steinberg in November of 1987 from a beating at the hands of a New York lawyer who adopted her illegally, a frightening story emerged. At least eight people noticed her disheveled look at school and at least five saw bruises on her face, arms, and back. But no one did anything. No investigation was made. No action was taken to get her away from the man who was brutalizing her. Society must hear the screams. See the signs. Take action to defend the defenseless.

Returning to the issue of abortion, unborn children have no voices of their own to raise. Society must have its conscience pricked on behalf of the one and one-half million babies who are aborted each year. Then, in cases where laws can be changed or where a woman can be encouraged to carry an unwanted pregnancy to term, society must help mothers and babies with health care, education, and the chance for a future. It is not a moral victory to discourage abortion and then to turn away from the problems which will be created by 1.5 million more mothers with 1.5 million more babies.

Communities must elect officials who will support not only programs to protect voting senior citizens but also children as well. Create school and community programs designed to protect young people from drugs, alcohol, and sexual exploitation. Close "adult bookstores" and massage parlors. Put the corner markets selling beer to minors out of business. These are minimal things which cities and towns across this nation can and should do to protect its children.

Second, the church has to accept some responsibility for the welfare of young people. If society as a whole has a

53

protective role to take concerning its children, the church can move beyond that to *provide a wholesome environment* for their spiritual development.

The church should provide acceptance and community for young people. In a word, children need to feel the same warmth, acceptance, and security in the presence of Christ's church that they felt in Jesus' personal presence. They should feel wanted, loved, and safe.

Ultimate answers for our children's needs cannot be provided by government. Just arresting drug pushers isn't enough. Closing porn shops is only a step in the right direction. Even taking children away from abusive parents isn't adequate. These young people who are trying to find a way to integrate themselves into life's mainstream must see something positive which can involve them. So let's get busy building churches where God's presence is felt and where love is experienced in significant, life-changing ways. Instead of scolding kids for their tastes in clothing or screaming for them to turn down their music, let's show them that the way of Jesus Christ is exciting enough that they will want to commit themselves to him.

We need to affirm our children when they are around us in church settings. If you are teaching children in a Bible class, study your Bible lesson; prepare your crafts and activities well. But when you get in there, devote time and attention to the children. Touch them. Especially the sad-looking ones. Hold them in your lap. If one of them is upset, hold that child in your arms the whole class time if that's what it takes to communicate Jesus to that girl or boy.

When these young people become teenagers, let them be themselves. Don't try to make them as dull and boring in their lifestyle as some of us have learned to be over 40, 50, or 60 years. Let some of their excitement infect the church. Insist that the teaching and ministry of the church be practical to real life, for otherwise young people will tune

54

it out and turn it off. Then we will wonder what happened to them when they "drop out of church."

Third, families certainly have a primary responsibility to their children. In a word, parents need to learn how to *nurture children.*

Nurturing children in the things of Christ (cf. Eph. 6:4) consists of three elements. Love, limits, and letting go.

Parents need to learn to love our children the way God has loved us. Unconditionally. Without reservation. For who they are rather than for what they do.

Hug your children. Comfort your children. Praise your children. When people come to your house and pay attention to your children, let that be your cue to let your children know how proud of them you are. Brag on them. Tell your guests how much you love them and how important they are in your life. Take a page out of the Heavenly Father's book and say, "This is my beloved son/daughter in whom I am well pleased." Translate those biblical words into your vocabulary at your house, and you will be amazed at the result.

When you have to disapprove of something your child has done or punish for wrongdoing, do so by disapproving and punishing the behavior and not the person. There is nothing inconsistent at all about scolding a child or even spanking a child for doing something and immediately afterwards picking that child up in your arms and holding her, telling her you love her, and affirming how proud you are of her. In fact, that helps communicate the message that what you disapprove of is not the child but what the child did. It's because you love her and believe that she is a good person that you're convinced that what she did is something she will never do again.

Then there is the matter of setting limits. There have to be boundaries for life. Since you are a Christian, live within the boundaries of Christian experience and Christian values. Respect for other people. Telling the truth. Respect for God's name and all that is holy. Let your children see your personal commitment to basic Christian values by the way you treat them and others.

Your children will challenge you at times. They will push against the boundaries you have set. They will see just how serious you are with your values. Don't overlook those challenges.

Your children are not evil when they challenge the boundaries you have defined. It is a part of their process of growing up. Just be consistent and unmoved from what you have taught and modeled. If their role is to test, your role is to stand firm. It is your job to say, "No, this is a limit beyond which we don't go in this family. . . . That language isn't used in this house. . . . You don't treat your mother that way. . . . We live within our means in our family."

Don't try to have a rule for everything. Keep the number of rules low, and keep their explanations simple. Let them be clearly understood. And then insist that everyone in the family live within them. No exceptions. No favoritism. No double standard.

Then, as children get older and more mature, parents have to do the hardest thing of all. We have to let go.

As your child grows older, give increasing amounts of accountability, expect it to be handled responsibly, and don't exempt him from failure. Don't hang over her shoulder. Don't do it for him if it doesn't get done. Let your children know the sweet success of doing something well. Let them taste the disappointment of failing at something. We grow from trying, failing, and learning from our mistakes. That's how you learned. Succeeding at some things. Failing at others. That's how your children will grow up.

Don't make emotional cripples out of your children by not letting them grow up. By not letting them make some decisions. Take some responsibility. Even once in a while fall on their face. Let them clean up their own messes, with

56

your love, guidance, and support. It is important for them to learn how real life is while still with you at home. Otherwise the world will be too cruel and too forbidding for them.

Conclusion

"Children are a gift from the Lord," says the Word of God. "Babies are a reward" (Psa. 127:3, The Everyday Bible). Since children come from God, their parents need to feel a strong sense of spiritual responsibility to them. Feed and clothe them. Educate them. Buy them toys. Above all else, though, teach them of God.

Let the name of Jesus be one of the first words your baby learns. When you begin reading to her, let her hear the stories of the Bible. Let your little boy learn to trust God the Father and to appreciate God's love which is as tender as a mother's and as strong as a father's. Teach your children that they belong to God rather than to you, for that is the truth of the matter. You are only stewards for God of these tender, teachable children.

Let your children hear you pray for them. Call their names to God. Thank God for them in their presence and for them to hear. Ask God to meet needs in their lives that you know about. Plead for him to deliver them from harm, from temptation, and from sin.

Make your home into a secure place where your child can grow. Let her make the bobbles of immaturity without being humiliated and punished for simply being a child. Let him ask childish questions without laughing at him or making fun of him. Brag on the good things you see in your child. When you have to correct or punish, deal with the behavior without demeaning the person.

Link your home with the church. Let worship, Bible study, class picnics, service projects, and family fellowship with other believers be regular experiences for the entire family. Give them priority over the dozens of things that will interrupt your involvement with the body of Christ if you let them.

Jesus loves the little children. And we can be the vehicles of that love in the orientation of their lives to all that is holy, good, and spiritual.

For Reflection and Discussion

1. What was the general situation with children and their protection in ancient cultures? What is *infanticide*? Why was it practiced in some societies?

2. What is the current status of abortion laws in the United States? What is the chief argument pressed by pro-abortion groups? What is the primary argument made by anti-abortion groups?

3. What are the latest statistics you can find about child abuse in this country?

4. In addition to abortion and abuse, this chapter also talks about our society's *absence* from its children. What does the term mean in this context? How does it influence children?

5. How does Luke demonstrate his interest in children in writing the third Gospel?

6. What events with children in Jesus' life did Luke include in his Gospel? What is the meaning and significance of *monogenes* when used of a son or daughter?

7. Explain what is meant in this chapter by a "conspiracy against childhood." Do you agree that it is a reality?

8. How can our society better fulfill its responsibility to protect the children among us?

9. Name some specific things the church should do to provide a good environment for the spiritual development of children.

10. What can families do to make their home environment better for the children there?

Chapter 5

Jesus and the Poor

Jesus of Nazareth was a poor man. Given the standard of living for most of the people who will read these lines, there's not much similarity between us and Jesus on a material level.

Seen through the eyes of a second-generation disciple who was Greek, the life our Savior lived as a Jew among Jews was hardly glamorous. Neither then nor now would he have been featured on *Lifestyles of the Rich and Famous*. Jesus was born in an animal shelter (2:6-7). The purification offering made by Joseph and Mary when Jesus was 40 days old was that allowed in the Torah for people too poor to afford a lamb (2:24, cf. Lev. 12:6-8).

All four Gospels depict Jesus as a member of the poorer class. He was a rabbi who received no pay for his teaching and was without visible means of support. In fact, words from his own mouth claimed, "Foxes have holes and birds of the air have nests, but the Son of Man has no place to lay his head" (9:58).

During his public ministry of three and a half years, Jesus' personal needs appear to have been met principally by the generosity of people who showed compassion to him as a friend and rabbi. There were some women who travelled with Jesus and supported him out of their resources (8:1-3). They evidently bought and prepared food during part of his ministry. Maybe during all of it. Perhaps they met other financial needs that he and the apostles encountered. He would occasionally be with friends like Lazarus, Mary, and Martha, and they would invite him into their home.

On most nights, however, Jesus apparently went to sleep without a roof over his head. He may have gone to sleep on an empty stomach on most of those same nights. According to the records left to us, he lived as a typical peasant of Palestine. This would mean that saving money and planning for retirement were never of concern to him. Each day brought its own challenge of finding the meals he would need to sustain himself.

Thus reminded that Jesus was a poor man, we must warn ourselves against creating churches that have no place for the people who are most like him insofar as wealth, assets, and influence are concerned.

Luke's Awareness of the Poor

Luke exhibited a tremendous amount of personal concern for the poor. It is, of course, beyond us to give a full account of that personal consciousness.

Reflecting on the man and his background, a likely source of his personal awareness comes to mind quickly. One suspects it relates to the fact of his profession. Luke was a doctor. Who knows the secrets of families and the way things are with them better than the trusted physician who goes into their homes? Luke's practice would not have been focused on a clean hospital and its census of patients but on people where they lived.

Dr. Luke is bound to have gone into many a home to assist in the birth of babies. Given the high infant mortality among people of his time, many of those infants didn't survive. Luke must have known that many of those babies died because their mothers had not had enough nourishment to sustain both them and the infants they were carrying. Luke is bound to have lost a lot of babies (and their mothers!) at delivery that he knew should not have been lost. And the problem was not his lack of medical skills. These people had just been so poor that they had been malnourished; a mother and her baby had not been able to live from the meager supply of food that had been available to the family.

Luke would also have tried to treat children who had diseases that resulted from malnutrition. Many diseases are directly associated with poverty even today. Take tuberculosis as a case in point. Do you have any friends who have had tuberculosis? Probably not. Most of us aren't put in situations where this infection threatens us. Yet a great many homeless people have tuberculosis. It relates directly to poverty and the life circumstance in which they live.

Luke must have seen so much of that. With his training as a physician, even though it was minimal by modern standards, he would have agonized over the fact that much of what he saw related to the lack of decent shelter or hygiene. It must have grieved him to see people who lacked basic food and nourishment. Luke was concerned about the poor, and so he talked about a lot of things from the life of Jesus that relate to his concern for the poor.

Luke was drawn to Jesus as one who knew poverty through his own experience. As one who taught about the relative meanings of wealth and poverty. As one who accepted some and rebuked others without regard to their economic status.

If we are Christ's spiritual presence in this world, we cannot be unconcerned about the poor. Somewhere between the *crackdown policies* of the political right and the *giveaway tendencies* of the political left, there is a place for God's people to stand in the breech to love and care for all people.

This sort of emphasis is not "social gospel" but integrity with the social implications of the gospel. The front line in dealing with those issues does not belong to government or to secular charities. God has assigned these concerns to people who wear the name of his Son. When we talk about "the poor and the homeless," we must remind ourselves that we are talking about *people*. People who live among us very much as Jesus lived among the people of his day.

Luke's Perspective on Jesus and the Poor

In the Gospel of Luke, a great deal is said about wealth and poverty. What is contained there serves both to comfort the afflicted and to afflict the comfortable.

In Mary's lovely song which anticipated the birth of Jesus, she celebrated God's concern for the poor and the lowly (1:51-53). The Son of God was born of humble parents and in circumstances of authentic poverty (2:6-7, 22-24). Humble shepherds were given the first notice of his birth and were the first visitors to see the newborn child (2:8-20).

The first event of Jesus' public ministry which Luke describes in detail was a synagogue sermon at Nazareth (4:14-30). It almost seems to be a broad outline of the messianic agenda for him. Thus it is all the more significant that Luke begins with Jesus reading a text from the prophet Isaiah which begins with these words: "The Spirit of the Lord is on me, because he has anointed me to preach good news to the poor." Luke understood Jesus' ministry as one to the poor. It was not merely one that would tolerate poor people as participants but which would make them the direct objects of his concern.

Furthermore, we might think of the significance of the Nazareth sermon in still another way. If you and I were going to search the Old Testament for prophecies about the life and work of the Messiah, we might pick texts about his birth, his relationship to David, or his miracles. But what text did Jesus choose from the Old Testament to serve as a prophetic anticipation of his work? It was one which affirmed that the gospel would be preached to the poor. The people who have never been sought out or given attention are going to be central to the mission of Jesus!

In the Sermon on the Plain, Jesus' first woe was to the rich (6:24) and his first blessing was to the poor (6:20). In the Parable of the Great Banquet, the host sent his servants to "bring in the poor, the crippled, the blind and the lame" (14:21b). The story of the rich man whose name is not even given and poor Lazarus reveals that one's status with regard to material things is not a reliable index to his spiritual situation (16:19-31).

Although Mark had already written down the story, Luke could not resist telling again about a certain widow and her gift (21:1-4; cf. Mark 12:41-44). While not a rebuke of those who could give large gifts, this story does rebuke giving to be seen of men. It is primarily a story which stresses the beauty of a gift which would be given out of poverty by one whose heart was devoted to God.

Neither Luke nor the Savior whose life he studied so closely ever pronounced an anathema on people who were wealthy; judgment was against those who put their trust in their riches and forgot God (cf. Prov. 11:28). On the other hand, neither Luke nor Jesus ever gave a benediction to people at the bottom of the socio-economic ladder as a class; these people were not to be disenfranchised from the Kingdom of God because of their situation. Returning to the rich man and Lazarus, the former was lost because of his spiritual insensitivity rather than because of his wealth; the latter was not denied the kingdom because he lived in such abject poverty among men.

Lest someone get the impression that the kingdom admitted no one of substance, Luke not only never condemns the possession of material goods but also shows that righteous people can use their prosperity to God's glory (8:1-3). Zacchaeus, although a rich man in a profession with a bad reputation, could be saved; then, once saved, he pledged half his wealth to helping the poor (19:1-9).

Luke records some key teachings of Jesus about the attitude Jesus wants his disciples to take toward material possessions.

In Luke 12:13-34 is found the Parable of the Rich Fool. It is the story of a man who says, "I've had a great crop year. So what am I going to do? I'll just build bigger barns!" Jesus says, "Fool! Tonight you're going to die, and none of these things you have planned to hoard will be worth anything to you again. Your life doesn't consist in the abundance of things you possess." It is that final line we are supposed to remember: *Life is not to be judged on the basis of possessions or the lack of them.*

In Luke 14:12-14, there is one of the most interesting statements that you'll find anywhere in the Gospels.

> Then Jesus said to his host, "When you give a luncheon or dinner, do not invite your friends, your brothers, or your relatives, or your rich neighbors; if you do, they may invite you back and so you will be repaid. But when you give a banquet, invite the poor, the crippled, the lame, the blind, and you will be blessed. Although they cannot repay you, you will be repaid at the resurrection of the righteous."

The point here is not that we can't have friends or that it is wrong to reciprocate kindnesses. The point is that we can't live just at that level. The Lord's people are sensitive people who would never limit their kindnesses to some rule of being generous only to those who can be generous in return. More than that, they imitate Jesus with regard to the poor: *Christians make the poor direct objects of their concern and kindness.*

The Poor Are With Us Still

For all the social programs and political promises which have been made in recent years, poverty is still a reality in our world.

On a visit to Nairobi in 1986, I went with a missionary and a physician into the Methare Valley, a slum area which was said to cover more than three square miles. There was one water hydrant to serve the entire area and not one toilet. Families lived in tiny one-room shacks made of cardboard, scraps of tin, or saplings plastered with mud. We went into the home of one Christian whose wife had died while giving birth to twins. The husband makes chairs and sells them for the equivalent of about 25 cents. Because there was no mother to care for or nurse the babies and because he couldn't provide formula, one of the babies had already died. Lydia, the surviving twin, was so malnourished that her tiny skeleton was distinct through her tissue-thin skin. The two cases of infant formula I bought her from my food money made some short-term difference in her case, but what is that against the total need which was (and still is) there? Her father is a good man. A hard-working man. But he lives in a circumstance of poverty which he did not create and from which he cannot escape.

Many of the children of India's "Untouchables" are put to work as beasts of burden in brick factories. As early as age eight, children are separated from their families for seven months of the year, no holidays, no weekends, no days of rest. They earn 15 rupees (about 75 cents) for every 1,000 bricks (at five and one-half pounds per brick) they transport.

When my wife and I were in London for our twenty-fifth anniversary and first honeymoon, our flight home left in the early morning so we had to get up early. We ate breakfast at the break of day beside a restaurant window in the nice hotel where we had stayed. I glanced out, saw someone, and said, "Myra, look. A lady's making up her bed." Just across the street in a recessed doorway, a woman was collecting a stack of newspapers that she had spread on concrete to keep the cold from coming directly against her body and putting them into a garbage bin. We had difficulty finishing breakfast as she started her day by stuffing her blanket into a plastic garbage bag, raising her dress, and relieving herself on the street.

Yes, you say, it is terrible that these conditions exist in Nairobi, India, and London. But they exist in my city of

Nashville as well. Right in the middle of the affluence of every city and town in America. And in the Appalachian Mountains. A Census Bureau report released near the end of 1989 found that 13.1 percent of citizens in the United States were in poverty.

Who are these poor people? How did they come to be in their situation? What is our responsibility to them?

Some people are in poverty due to their sins of extravagance or laziness. The Scripture acknowledges as much in passages such as Proverbs 6:6-11; 10:4; 19:15; and 24:30-34. Others are there because of alcoholism or drug addiction (Prov. 23:19-35).

Some people are out there because they're mentally ill, and they have fallen through the cracks of our healthcare network or social-services system. And, strange as it may sound to you, studies show that some people are homeless and living on the streets because they choose to be there; they have families and job skills, but they choose to live on the streets.

For some of these people (e.g., lazy men), it is difficult to feel sympathy, although some of them have wives and children they have dragged into their circumstance. For others (e.g., mentally ill persons), there may be sympathy but a feeling of helplessness about how to change "The System" to meet their needs.

Yet it is very important for us to realize that the problem of poverty (and our responsibility to do something about it!) cannot be dismissed by lumping everyone into the groups just identified. There are hundreds of thousands of people living below the poverty line by no fault of their own.

There are down-on-their-luck ordinary people living in poverty in the United States. Single mothers. Dads laid off or let go from closed plants. People who want to work but who are disabled by injury or sickness.

Then there is the category known as "the working poor." This includes households where wage earners work either full- or part-time during the year but still have incomes below the official poverty line. While the number of welfare poor has risen moderately during the past decade, the number of working poor has mushroomed. While welfare poor are led by city dwellers, minorities, and female-headed households, the working poor divide about evenly among cities, suburbs, and rural areas and the majority are white, two-parent families. In other words, the stereotypes of poverty don't reflect reality very well.

These people feel such shame at living in poverty. They know the public perception of who they are and why they are in distress. And it strips away their dignity and self-esteem.

Scripture reflects a more enlightened and sympathetic posture toward the poor than some of us have taken. Poverty is regarded as an involuntary social evil which is to be assaulted rather than tolerated. "He who mocks the poor shows contempt for their Maker" (Prov. 17:5a); "He who is kind to the poor lends to the Lord" (Prov. 19:17a).

Jesus was poor and identified with the poor, handicapped, and hungry in his ministry; he taught that in feeding the hungry, clothing the naked, and welcoming the homeless his disciples would be ministering to him (Matt. 25:35-40). The New Testament epistles teach that Christians are to relieve widows and orphans (Jas. 1:27) and "do good to all people" (Gal. 6:10).

The Gospel of Luke shows that the Gentile physician who had a sense of social justice was drawn to Jesus in part by the compassion of the Jewish Savior he confessed to be the Son of God and Savior of the World. One cannot help thinking that more people of any generation or culture would be drawn to Jesus if his people were more active in doing the things that he did among the poor and powerless.

Conclusion

The poor are still here, and Jesus said they always would be. But they are here and always will be here because the world is flawed, cursed, and sinful. They are *not* here because it is the will of God that they should exist and their numbers swell.

The frontline responsibility for dealing with poverty, hunger, and other compassion issues does not belong to government agencies or charitable enterprises of a secular variety. God has marked that spot for his own people, and we must take it to heart that he expects us to exhibit in our lives the same compassion that motivated Jesus.

For Reflection and Discussion

1. Define the lifestyle of Jesus from what we know of it through the Gospels.

2. What do you think of the speculation that much of Luke's interest in the poor grew out of his profession? Is this a reasonable supposition?

3. Distinguish the "social gospel" from the "social implications of the gospel."

4. Summarize the teachings of Jesus about wealth and poverty found in the Gospel of Luke.

5. What is the point of the parable found at Luke 12:13-34?

6. Study the statement of Jesus recorded at Luke 14:12-14. How are we supposed to interpret and apply what he said?

7. Many people are in poverty due to laziness, alcoholism, or other "sinister" reasons. Have you ever heard anyone dismiss poor and homeless people generally by using these reasons to account for all poverty? Using epithets like "bums" or "worthless trash" to describe all poor and homeless people? How do you respond?

8. How does the Old Testament treat the issue of poverty and people suffering from its effects? Do some research on specific provisions made for the relief of the poor in the Old Testament.

9. Describe Jesus' relationship to poverty. To poor people. To the relief of the poor. Is the rest of the New Testament consistent with his teaching and example?

10. In light of the ongoing problem of poverty (cf. Deut. 15:11; Matt. 26:11), what are some practical things the church can do to address the needs of people? What should we be doing about warning others of the danger of their prosperity?

Chapter 6

The Holy Spirit in Luke

Christians understand that our world of human experience has been not only created at the hand of God but also entered into by deity. The abiding agent of that contact between humankind and the Godhead is variously called in Scripture the Spirit, the Holy Spirit, the Spirit of God, or the Spirit of Christ.

The earliest Christians were acutely aware of the Holy Spirit at work among them.

> Whereas other religions saw a divine spirit as coming on only a few especially important people, Christians realized that God's Spirit comes on all believers. And whereas pagans thought that the presence of the divine spirit was to be known by various forms of ecstatic behavior, Christians knew his presence by his 'fruit' in ethical conduct."[1]

The early church affirmed that the Holy Spirit had come on every follower of Jesus Christ and that every Christian is a depository of the Holy Spirit. Its members believed that every baptized believer in Jesus Christ had been given the "gift of the Holy Spirit" (Acts 2:38) and that his or her body was a place the Spirit of God personally lived (1 Cor. 6:19). Perhaps the lack of awareness of and lack of dependence on the Holy Spirit is the most glaring difference in believers now when compared with the first-century church.

Luke shows more concern for the activity of the Holy Spirit among the people of God than any other Gospel writer. He refers to the Spirit 17 times, as compared with 12

[1] Leon Morris, *New Testament Theology* (Grand Rapids: Zondervan Publishing House, 1986), p. 191.

times for Matthew and six for Mark. Thus we are justified in taking this as one of those topics in which Luke had a special interest and in attempting to discover why it constituted a "selling point" for this Greek writer who was trying to bring others like himself to believe in a Jewish man as the Savior of All.

In the course of our study, we will be seeking to understand why it is so important for us to live a spiritual (i.e., Spirit-filled, Spirit-controlled) life today.

Luke's Consciousness of the Holy Spirit

The third Gospel makes it clear that the Holy Spirit was central to the event of the Incarnation. When Gabriel foretold the birth of Jesus to Mary, she was confused. Her specific question of the angel was this: "How shall this be, since I am a virgin?" (1:34). Gabriel's answer focused on the involvement of the Holy Spirit. "The Holy Spirit will come upon you, and the power of the Most High will overshadow you" (1:35a).

Then, in the events designed to set the stage for the public ministry of Jesus of Nazareth, the Holy Spirit was active in the ministry of John the Baptist. John was filled with the Holy Spirit from his birth (1:15). His mother (1:41) and father (1:67) both prophesied by the Holy Spirit.

Even so, John indicated that part of the superiority of the Messiah's ministry would lie in the latter's ability to bestow the Spirit of God on others (3:16). Thus John was conscious of an empowerment by the Holy Spirit but also of his inability to impart either the person or power of the Spirit to others.

At the initiation of Jesus' public ministry, the Spirit came down on him in the visible form of a dove (3:21-22). This was certainly a sign of identification to John which confirmed the identity of Jesus to him. But was it not more? Was the descent of the Spirit not for the sake of Jesus as well

70

as for John's sake? Shall we not conclude that the Son of Man needed the full equipping of the Spirit's power for his ministry? Whatever growing sense of messianic awareness there had been in Jesus was now confirmed and sealed to him. The work which lay ahead for him was not a work to be undertaken in the resources and ingenuity of unaided humanity.

Luke ties together the words "spirit" (Gk, *pneuma*) and "power" (Gk, *dynamis*). Jesus was "full of the Holy Spirit" when led into the wilderness to be tempted by Satan (4:1). At the end of the ordeal, he is "in the power of the Spirit" (4:14). In fact, this expression describing him at the end of the temptation experience constitutes something of an additional contract between Jesus and John the Baptist. John was "in the spirit and power of *Elijah*" for the sake of performing his preliminary mission (1:17); Jesus alone, however, was "in the power of the *Spirit*" when accomplishing his work.

Luke sets the first public event of the ministry of Jesus in his boyhood home. He went to Nazareth where he had been brought up, and on the Sabbath day he went into the synagogue. Then, when he stood up to read, a significant thing happened.

> The scroll of the prophet Isaiah was handed to him. Unrolling it, he found the place where it is written: "The Spirit of the Lord is on me, because he has anointed me to preach good news to the poor." . . . Then he rolled up the scroll, gave it back to the attendant and sat down. The eyes of everyone in the synagogue were fastened on him, and he began by saying to them, "Today this scripture is fulfilled in your hearing" (4:17-21).

Have you followed the theme of these texts from Luke? The Spirit came on Jesus at his baptism; the same Spirit led him into the desert for 40 days of testing. At the end of the 40 days, Jesus came out of the desert "in the power of the Spirit." Then he went to Nazareth, read from the Isaiah scroll there, and said "the Spirit of the Lord is on me."

The Isaiah passage was fulfilled not only on that specific day in Nazareth but throughout his ministry. Then, at the end of his ministry, he promised "power from on high" to his disciples (24:49). Thus the *unique bearer* of the Holy Spirit became the *unique dispenser* of the Spirit to others. This promise of the Holy Spirit became the junction point for Luke's Gospel and the Acts.

From Luke's point of view, Christ's entire ministry was undergirded by the Holy Spirit. His ministry showed the power of the Spirit. It showed human experience being broken into by divine presence.

Human witnesses during that period of public ministry saw and heard things men had never seen or heard before. Jesus prophesied by the Spirit of God. He worked miracles with the Spirit of God. He healed blind eyes. He raised the dead. He walked on water. He multiplied food. A limited world had been broken into by an unlimited presence. The Spirit of God was present in Jesus.

The Role of the Holy Spirit

The Spirit of God is the Great Enabler of the people of God. On a Marxist view, religion is merely the "opiate of the masses." In biblical perspective, however, the Spirit of God is a dynamo rather than a narcotic, a helper rather than an excuse.

The "gift of the Holy Spirit" has been promised to all who have been baptized in Jesus' name (Acts 2:38). Paul affirmed that the body of a Christian is a "temple of the Holy Spirit who is in you" (1 Cor. 6:19; cf. Rom. 8:9-11; Gal. 4:6). Saved persons have a new relationship with the Spirit which did not exist before conversion.

The presence of the Holy Spirit constitutes a "seal" upon a believer. "Having believed, you were marked in him with a seal, the promised Holy Spirit..." (Eph. 1:13b; 4:30). The idea carried by this term involves an official stamping or marking of a thing to indicate its ownership. It also refers to the sort of authentication which a seal gives to a diploma or certificate. Thus the Holy Spirit is given to saved people to mark, claim, and authenticate those people who belong to God. Indeed, "if anyone does not have the Spirit of Christ, he does not belong to Christ" (Rom. 8:9).

The Holy Spirit serves his primary enabling role in a Christian's life by helping him overcome sin. How do converted men and women deal with the things which used to be their undoing? Things like lying, greed, or lust? Addictive behaviors such as chemical dependency? It is "by the Spirit" that Christians "put to death the misdeeds of the body" (Rom. 8:13). Yes, we still have to struggle. Any help or support available to us should be used. But the child of God has the promise that God will "strengthen you with power through his Spirit in your inner being" for these battles against the sinful nature (cf. Eph. 3:14-19).

There is also a role played by the Spirit of God in the prayer life of Christ's disciples. In times when one's heart is so weighed down that he cannot articulate his requests to God, the indwelling Spirit who knows the heart turns his sighs and groanings into eloquent intercession (cf. Rom. 8:26).

The very written Word of God we study for spiritual insight was produced by the Holy Spirit. He guided the prophets and apostles of the early church to record what was happening for our sakes, for our guidance. Scripture was given as the Holy Spirit moved men to produce it (2 Pet. 1:20-21). But the Holy Spirit is greater than the written word, and he has filled it with magnificent promises of personal involvement in our lives. Promises such as the ones just noted affirm that his power is active in Christians. By an increased awareness of him and through a conscious yieldedness to his presence, one becomes fruitful in the things of righteousness (cf. Gal. 5:22-23).

With our rationalistic bent, we want the Spirit to be confined to what the Spirit says. But the Spirit is no more confined in his personality and power to what he says than you are confined to your words. As a person, you are more than, greater than, and other than anything you say. In your person, you carry out the things you promise to do. But in doing that, you are more than and greater than the promises themselves. Similarly, the activity of the Holy Spirit in carrying out his commitments to believers goes beyond the Scripture which contains his words. While we can be certain that he will do nothing which contradicts what he has revealed in the Word of God, we can be equally sure that he does more than simply influence us as we read the Bible.

True Spirituality

Perhaps this is as good a place as any to raise the larger topic of *spirituality*. We sometimes refer to people we know as "spiritual" in their lifestyles. We sometimes express the desire for "more evidence of spirituality" in our own behavior. Do you realize that even to use the term "spiritual" or "spirituality" you are affirming something of the relationship of the Holy Spirit to you?

One who affirms a desire to live spiritually is really asking to know more of the presence, power, and enabling of the Holy Spirit in his or her life.

What is it, then, to be spiritual? True spirituality is perfectly illustrated by Mary (1:35-38). The normal time of arranging a marriage for a Jewish girl was in her mid-teens; the normal time for the marriage to occur would be well before her twentieth year. If we assume that this marriage had been arranged at the normal times, Mary was only a teenaged girl. Imagine her trying to understand what was thrown at her in that conversation.

The angel Gabriel spoke to her and told her that she had been selected to "be with child and give birth to a son" (1:31). That son was to "be great and will be called the Son of the Most High" (1:32a). Her response to this? "I am a virgin!" (1:34b). Mary was biologically literate enough to know that women do not have babies except as the result of sexual experience. And she was morally innocent enough to know it was not possible for her to be pregnant by a man. Not by her beloved Joseph, to whom she was engaged. Certainly not by anyone else.

So how will a teenaged girl deal with this sort of thing? "The Holy Spirit will come upon you, and the power of the Most High will overshadow you," said Gabriel. "So the holy one to be born will be called the Son of God" (1:35). Do you think she understood all that? How it would work in relation to Joseph, her own family, and gossipy neighbors? What it would mean to her total life? Of course not! She couldn't have made sense of what was happening, for what was happening was a miracle without precedent.

The late Francis Schaeffer has suggested three possible responses that Mary could have made to what she had heard. Number one was to say, "No way!" Sometimes when we are so frightened of things happening by means and ends that we don't understand, we just immediately back off and say, "I don't want any part in this. I don't understand this. Nothing like this has ever happened. I can just imagine all sorts of problems. What would Joseph think?"

Another possibility, equally extreme perhaps on the other side, would have been to say, "Wonderful! I'll claim this promise of God that I am to have a baby, and I'll go get Joseph and tell him that we don't have to wait the 12 months from our betrothal, and we can start living together today. I'll claim this promise and exert all my energy to make it come to pass." And she could have set about arranging the agenda by which God's work will be done. Hold on! How can she accomplish this by her own power?

The third possible response she could have made would have been to say, "I still don't understand what you're talking about. There is no precedent for this. There's nothing in Scripture about anything like this having ever happened before, and my mind whirrs at the possibility. Yet, if this promise is of God, I will be his handmaiden. I will be his servant. It will be as he has said."

It was the third response which Mary gave. "I am the Lord's servant," she said. Her final words to the angel were these: "May it be to me as you have said" (1:38).

This is the perfect precedent for everything that is spiritual. Today the church is the bride of Christ. Today the church has a mission that boggles our minds. The church has challenges that we don't know how to meet. Local churches have challenges and opportunities, even risks and perils. We pull our hair. We lose sleep. We think: Can we? Should we? Dare we?

It seems to me that we have three possible responses to anything that God has called us to do in this world. One is to resist it and say, "Because I don't know how it can be done, I will have no part in it." Possibility number two is to say, "Well, yes, I believe that it is of God; so I will do it in my own strength and by my own methods." Possibility number three is the one that is truly spiritual. It is to say that because we believe it is God's will we will commit ourselves to it. We will believe that there is a power at work in us to accomplish it that is greater than anything we know or any scheme we can devise. Then we yield ourselves as instruments for God to use in accomplishing his holy purposes.

Schaeffer calls Mary's response to God "active passivity."

There is an active passivity here. She took her own body, by choice, and put it into the hands of God to do the thing that he said he would do, and Jesus was born. She gave herself, with her body, to God. In response to the promise, yes; but not to do it herself. This is a beautiful, exciting personal expression of a relationship between a finite person and the God she loves. Now this is absolutely unique and must not be confused; there is only one virgin birth. Nevertheless, it is an illustration of our being the bride of Christ. We are in the same situation in that we have these great and thrilling promises we have been considering, and we are neither to think of ourselves as totally passive, as though we had no part in this, as though God had stopped dealing with us now as men; nor are we to think we can do it ourselves. If we are to bring forth fruit in the Christian life, or rather, if Christ is to bring forth this fruit through us by the agency of the Holy Spirit, there must be a constant act of faith, of thinking: Upon the basis of your promises I am looking for you to fulfill them, O my Jesus Christ; bring forth your fruit through me into this poor world.[2]

The role of the church in getting God's work done in this world, from the building of a church building to the evangelization of the world, is "active passivity." Passively, you and I admit that there is no way we can do it. Yet, because we believe the promise and the call are of God, we commit ourselves to allowing him to do it through us. Thus, actively, we commit ourselves to participation in God's work by yielding ourselves to involvement with his work in feeding the hungry, sharing the gospel, or whatever good work is at stake which will give God glory.

When the process is done, the power for its accomplishment is assigned to the Spirit of God. All the glory is given to God. We take no credit and make no boasts. The

[2] Francis A Schaeffer, *True Spirituality* (Wheaton, IL: Tyndale House Publishers, 1971), pp. 58-59.

basis for our confidence that God is still alive and working in this world is that such things still happen.

The only true evidence of the Spirit's power within a man or woman will be the external deeds he brings about. We are in a great cosmic struggle (cf. Eph. 6:11-12). The Holy Spirit lives within God's people as the internal *prod to* and *power for* good works. Acts of unselfish sacrifice. Gentleness. Love. Moment by moment, we are either being used by God in the power of his Holy Spirit or we are *resisting* and *grieving* the Spirit.

Conclusion

What does the Bible mean when it says that God will give direction in our times of confusion? That God will respond to our prayers by giving wisdom when we don't know which way to turn? What does the Bible mean when it says you won't be tempted above your ability to bear it? When it says you'll never be put in a situation from which there is no way of escape? What does the Bible mean by all these promises, and dozens of others that could be cited, unless it is this: Your world of limited means and resources has been broken into by a power you can't understand, and because you are mine I will fill you with that power. I will work in your life to accomplish my purposes. I will see you through every crisis and get you safely home to me at the end.

Something broken in your life? Something you've gone through that doesn't make sense? Why did this family break up? Why did the car accident occur? Why did the baby die? The promise of Scripture is not some rationalistic hope of insight to make sense of such things or to figure out how to keep more from occurring. The promise is that, because there is a new presence in human experience, you will not be destroyed by these things. The power that is in you is greater than the power that is in the world to work against you to destroy you. That is the mystery. At least, it is *part* of the mystery of the doctrine of the Holy Spirit.

In presenting a Jewish Savior to the larger Roman world, Luke affirmed the inscrutability of Christian faith. It is not a hokey, occult mysticism; it is the truth that God's work in this world is accomplished through an "active passivity" that permits the power of the Holy Spirit to produce fruit in the lives of believers such as us.

For Reflection and Discussion

1. In what ways did Luke tie the Holy Spirit to the event of the Incarnation? Why is this significant?

2. What interesting thing does Luke do with the words "spirit" and "power" in his Gospel?

3. Contrast the relationship John the Baptist had with the Holy Spirit and Jesus' relationship to the Spirit.

4. What is the relationship of the Holy Spirit to Christians today? Cite some New Testament texts about the partnership established between the Spirit and believers.

5. What is the primary role of the Holy Spirit as the Great Enabler? Read the quotation from Leon Morris on the first page of this chapter and reflect on it in light of this purpose.

6. What is the relationship between the Holy Spirit and the written Scriptures?

7. Define the word *spirituality*. What does it affirm about a relationship with the Holy Spirit?

8. Review the case study in Luke concerning Mary and her submission to God's announcement of the birth of her son. How does it exemplify true spirituality? Is Schaeffer's analysis helpful to you?

9. What does the term "active passivity" mean in the context of this chapter? Is the idea biblical? Is it practical? Do you know the concept through experience?

10. In what sense is there an inscrutable nature to Christian faith? Why do so many tend to withdraw from the idea that such a thing is so? Does rationalistic pride ever come into conflict with divine accomplishment in a human life?

Chapter 7

How to Make God Happy

Do you ever think of God in terms of his happiness? His pleasure? His joy?

God must have a wonderful sense of humor. Have you ever looked at a zebra? Ever thought about the architecture of a camel or a duck-billed platypus? They seem to me like pretty good evidence that God has a sense of humor. But you can look at this matter of the divine sense of humor in a different way.

With human beings, a healthy sense of humor keeps life in balance. The person who cannot laugh at his own foibles and those of others will get depressed and short-tempered. If God made no allowance for our fallibility and foolishness, he surely would have lost all patience with us aeons ago and melted the universe down to nothingness.

I can readily imagine that God smiles the wry grin of a knowing father as he observes the immature antics of his children. When he hears some of our prayers which are litanies of cliches. When he sees us drop less in a collection plate than we spent on a night out last week and call it giving. When we engage in fratricide and call it "contending for the faith." When we persist in addressing boring, irrelevant issues from our pulpits while hurting people in our audiences are dying for a word from God which speaks to their lives. Even these things, though, are not what I have in mind in this chapter in talking about God's happiness.

In speaking of the pleasure and joy of God in Luke's Gospel, one has to look at something more spiritually significant than a sense of humor or God's amusement over what a well-known hymn calls "our foolish ways."

Luke has a great deal to say about repentance and cites Jesus to the effect that *repentance gives God pleasure.*

When God sees someone in the process of turning his or her life away from things that have been destructive to it and beginning to seek right and holy things instead, he is happy.

Look at the parables of Luke 15. All three of them were given in response to grumbling by some of Jesus' critics that he was hanging around with the wrong crowd. He was eating with tax collectors and prostitutes. What was Jesus' response? He didn't argue with his detractors. He simply told them some stories. Each had the same "punch line."

> Suppose one of you has a hundred sheep and loses one of them. Does he not leave the ninety-nine in the open country and go after the lost sheep until he finds it? And when he finds it, he joyfully puts it on his shoulders and goes home. Then he calls his friends and neighbors together and says, "Rejoice with me; I have found my lost sheep." I tell you that in the same way, there will be more rejoicing in heaven over one sinner who repents than over ninety-nine righteous persons who do not need to repent (15:3-7).

Did you catch the line about "rejoicing in heaven over one sinner who repents"? A similar line is also contained in the second story.

> Or, suppose a woman has ten silver coins and loses one. Does she not light a lamp, sweep the house and search carefully until she finds it? And when she finds it, she calls her friends and neighbors together and says, "Rejoice with me; I have found my lost coin." In the same way, I tell you, there is rejoicing in the presence of the angels of God over one sinner who repents (15:8-10).

In both of these familiar parables, Jesus speaks of rejoicing in heaven when a sinner repents. In the second story, there is "rejoicing in the presence of the angels." The expression duplicates the ending of the chapter's former parable about "rejoicing in heaven." We are being told yet another time that the thing which causes happiness to radiate outward from the central throne to every angel who serves its occupant is the rescue of a sinner from Satan's clutches. When someone who has been lost and in danger is rescued from peril, there is a celebration in heaven. It is the sort of thing which happens when loving concern gives way to relief.

What makes God happy? The Bible says God is happy when he sees lives turned around. When God sees a lost sheep brought back into the fold. When God sees a lost coin put back where it belongs.

Then, of course, there is a third story in the same chapter that Jesus told his critics. It is probably the best-known story in all literature. The Parable of the Prodigal Son (15:11-32) portrays a father running to his penitent son. Hugging and kissing him. Throwing a party. Get the point? Since the father in this parable unquestionably represents the Father in heaven, it underscores even more emphatically the point made by the first two stories. *Repentance makes God happy.*

Luke's Emphasis on Repentance

One of the theological distinctives in the Gospel of Luke is its explicit emphasis on repentance in the teaching of Jesus. This is not to deny that repentance is an issue of importance in the other Gospels or in other parts of the New Testament. But the materials written by Paul's physician-friend underscore the necessity of repentance more emphatically than any other. The noun "repentance" (Gk, *metanoia*) occurs 22 times in the New Testament; exactly half these occurrences are in Luke's writings. The verb "repent" (Gk, *metanoeo*) appears 14 of its total of 34 times in his writings.

Take the Synoptics as a case study. Matthew, Mark, and Luke all quote Jesus as saying, "I have not come to call the righteous, but sinners." Only Luke, however, adds "to repentance" (5:32). Thus what is implicit in Matthew and Mark is made explicit in Luke.

Luke tells of Jesus' remorse over the failure of his generation to repent. In Luke 10:13, Luke preserves an account of Jesus talking about two Jewish cities in Galilee, Chorazin and Bethsaida. Jesus speaks of these two cities to rebuke his generation's hardheartedness. "For if the miracles that were performed in you had been performed in Tyre and Sidon," he said, "they would have repented long ago, sitting in sack cloth and ashes."

In the next chapter, Luke records a much broader statement about repentance from the Son of God. In a sweeping judgment against his whole generation, he predicted a terrible fate for those who continued to harden their hearts against God. "The men of Nineveh will stand up at the judgment with this generation and condemn it," he insisted, "for they repented at the preaching of Jonah, and now one greater than Jonah is here" (11:32).

Luke also develops a very interesting and practical attitude toward misfortune in human experience. He avoids the trap of seeing all suffering as the judgment of God against people. Yet he evidently believes that tragedy can get our attention as nothing else can, prompt sober reflection, and lead to repentance over personal sin. His approach anticipated John Donne's reflection on the ringing of a church bell to signal someone's death. "It tolls for thee," he wrote.

This perspective comes through in his record of Jesus' reaction to a couple of events known to him. One day some people told Jesus about some "Galileans whose blood Pilate had mixed with their sacrifices" (13:1). We know nothing of this episode beyond this reference. Perhaps Pilate had sent soldiers in on a group of Jewish worshippers at a festival in Jerusalem. He responded, "Do you think that these Galileans were worse sinners than all the other

Galileans because they suffered this way? I tell you, no! But unless you repent, you too will all perish" (13:2-3). In other words, against the tendency of some to see the fate of those poor Galileans as a judgment from God, Jesus denied that it was so. But the contemplation of such tragic events ought to move sensitive persons to take stock of their own lives and to repent.

Then Jesus turned the group's attention to a construction accident which had apparently been discussed widely. "Or those eighteen who died when the tower in Siloam fell on them," he said, "do you think they were more guilty than all the others living in Jerusalem?" (13:4). Lest someone answer in the affirmative, he continued, "I tell you, no! But unless you repent, you too will all perish" (13:5).

What is the message to you from every funeral you attend? You are vulnerable. You do not have a perpetual lease on life. So you must be prepared for death always and for the reckoning with God which follows it. People who live through hurricanes, earthquakes, or serious illnesses often speak of "seeing things more clearly now" or "getting their priorities right" from what they have gone through. Luke would not have any of us miss lessons such as these, whether from our own experiences or from those of others.

What is Repentance?

Perhaps the nature of repentance needs to be pursued more directly at this point in our study. Just what is it? How does one experience and express it?

Repentance is not the same thing as fear. Many people get scared by financial problems or health crises who never change anything.

Neither is it a matter of regret and promising to do better, because millions of frightened people have made many promises in hospital rooms and corridors who have never repented.

Repentance is not even confession, because sometimes a person confesses only because he has been caught with his hand in the cookie jar. Thus he confesses, not because of conscience and spiritual sensitivity, but because he has been caught and cannot deny his guilt.

Repentance is not paying a penalty to someone. People sometimes have to pay penalties under law. Thus they pay fines. Do public service. Serve time in prison. But sometimes their hearts don't really seem to be touched, and they don't change. They go back to their old ways and become repeat offenders within the system.

And it is probably important for us to understand that religion isn't repentance. It wasn't in Jesus' day. The very people who he said didn't understand how to repent were people who were devoutly religious. Remember what the Lord said to them? "Harlots and publicans will go into the kingdom before you." We should not fool ourselves into thinking that anyone who is a churchgoer must therefore understand about repentance.

Repentance, while it may involve elements of all these, is deeper and encompasses more. It may involve fear. It may involve paying a penalty. It may involve confession, and it may involve making some promises. But repentance is much, much more. Repentance is a fuller response to God than any of those things.

Two texts in the Gospel of Luke point to the nature of genuine repentance.

The first one concerns the ministry of John the Baptist. In Luke's Gospel, John's work is an integral part of Jesus' ministry. John preached a baptism of repentance. "He went into all the country around the Jordan, preaching a baptism of repentance for the forgiveness of sins" (3:3). He called for the people coming to receive his baptism to produce "fruit in keeping with repentance" (3:8). Fortunately for the sake of our understanding, Luke records their request for John to explain the demand and his answer.

To the crowd in general, he said, "The man with two tunics should share with him who has none, and the one who has food should do the same" (3:11). To some tax collectors, he said, "Don't collect any more than you are required to" (3:13). To some soldiers wanting to know the meaning of repentance, he said, "Don't extort money and don't accuse people falsely -- be content with your pay" (3:14b).

There is a second story in the Gospel of Luke that details repentance. It's that third parable from Luke 15 which was mentioned earlier. After telling about a lost sheep and a lost coin, Jesus told the story of a lost boy. In that story, repentance is traced out in the boy's behavior.

> There was a man who had two sons. The younger one said to his father, "Father, give me my share of the estate." So he divided his property between them.
>
> Not long after that, the younger son got together all he had, set off for a distant country and there squandered his wealth in wild living. After he had spent everything, there was a severe famine in that whole country, and he began to be in need. So he went and hired himself out to a citizen of that country, who sent him to his fields to feed pigs. He longed to fill his stomach with the pods that the pigs were eating, but no one gave him anything.
>
> When he came to his senses, he said, "How many of my father's hired men have food to spare, and here I am starving to death! I will set out and go back to my father and say to him: Father, I have sinned against heaven and against you. I am no longer worthy to be called your son; make me like one of your hired men." So he got up and went to his father.
>
> But while he was still a long way off, his father saw him and was filled with compassion for him. He ran to his son, threw his arms around him and kissed him.
>
> The son said to him, "Father, I have sinned against heaven and against you. I am no longer worthy to be called your son."

> But the father said to his servants, "Quick!
> Bring the best robe and put it on him. Put a ring on
> his finger and sandals on his feet. Bring the fattened
> calf and kill it. Let's have a feast and celebrate. For
> this son of mine was dead and is alive again; he was
> lost and is found." So they began to celebrate
> (15:11-24).

What is repentance? In this story, it is defined in terms of *realization* (15:17), when the boy comes to his senses. Here's a boy who has been at home with his father. He gets restless. He feels a stirring of rebellion. So he asks for and receives his part of the estate. He goes off and wastes it. And then he comes to his senses. The first step to repentance is realization of the mess you're in. What you've done. Personal ownership of responsibility for it. Taking the blame for your behavior.

The second step is *remorse* (15:17). "When he came to his senses, he said, 'How many of my father's hired men have food to spare, and here I am starving to death!' " There's remorse. There's grief. There's pain. When you have made a mess of your life, you have also caused your life to be undone and out of place and out of harmony with your father.

The third step of repentance in this story involves a *resolve* (15:18). "I will set out and go back to my father and say to him: 'Father, I have sinned against heaven and against you.' "

But a resolve is no good without a *reformation*. An actual change of behavior. In verse 20, after the formation of a holy resolve and determination, the text says: "So he got up and went to his father." It wasn't just a good intention of what he ought to do. His repentance meant that he actually got up, pointed his face toward home, and began moving in his father's direction.

There's even a fifth item that frequently belongs in the total process called repentance. It doesn't appear in the story of the prodigal son because it doesn't seem to have been possible for him. Where it is possible, however, it should be done. This fifth element is *restitution*. One of the most painful things about repentance is that restitution is not always possible. Perhaps it is even correct to say that it is rarely possible. Putting things back as they were. Restoring what was taken. Setting the record straight. It seems apparent that restitution is the natural fruit of repentance. When it is possible to do something to put things back right again, repentance acts to perform the deed.

Satan has an alternative to repentance, however. His response to sinful behavior begins with *refusal*. You just refuse to admit your blame. You deny any responsibility for the mess. The second step is *rationalization*. You explain why what you did really wasn't so bad after all. It certainly wasn't so bad as what somebody else you know did. The third move is *ridicule*. That is, you start blaming everybody else. It's somebody else's fault that you got in this mess. You're not really responsible. The fourth response is *resistance* to any sort of change in your life. That, in turn, guarantees the fifth step of *repetition*. You'll do it again. You'll go right back. You'll wallow in the same pig pen from which God offers you an escape.

The difference between repentance and Satan's alternative to it is apparent. Repentance results in a changed attitude, commits one to a new behavior, and sends one directly to God. The satanic substitute for repentance evades responsibility, defends the old behavior, and flees the presence of God.

Repentance is fundamentally a judgment about ourselves. In fact, we are in danger of trivializing repentance when we "repent *of something*" rather than simply "*repent*." Most often the Bible just talks about *repentance*.

That is, our fundamental need is not to stop this deed or to begin this behavior. Our most basic need is to accept the Bible's judgment on ourselves as sinners who are unable

89

to please God. To admit our powerlessness before sin. Why do you think Jesus kept telling church-goers that harlots would enter the kingdom before them? They judge themselves unfit and helpless and turn to Christ for help.

The Urgency of This Theme

Repentance is not a take-it-or-leave-it option in Christian experience. It is fundamental and essential. There is no way to affirm love for God and righteousness while denying the demands of repentance. Consider this quote from the late A. W. Tozer:

> When will Christians learn that to love righteousness it is necessary to hate sin? that to accept Christ it is necessary to reject self? that to follow the good way we must flee from evil? that a friend of the world is an enemy of God? that God allows no twilight zone between two altogethers where the fearful and the doubting may take refuge at once from hell to come and the rigors of present discipline?[1]

There's no choice between the two. No "twilight zone between two altogethers." If you wish to take refuge from hell, then, the discipline of repentance is a mandate from God that cannot be escaped. There is no third alternative. As another writer has put it:

> The fact is, repentance is a missing note in much modern evangelism. The appeal is not for repentance, but for enlistment. Birth defects are not only medical, but spiritual. Many ills of the Christian life are due to handicapped beginnings. Too many people are preaching a warped or truncated gospel, and spiritual birth defects are the inevitable result.[2]

[1] A. W. Tozer, *That Incredible Christian* (Harrisburg, PA: Christian Publications, 1964), p. 76.
[2] J. Edwin Orr, "Playing the Good News Melody Off-key," *Christianity Today* (Jan. 1, 1982): 25.

Well said. It *isn't* enough to be enlisted. It isn't enough to raise your hand and say that you are on the Lord's side. Before you can be his, you have to repent. You have to pass a judgment against yourself before you can come to the Lord for salvation and cleansing. No, you have to agree with the divine judgment on all humanity: "There is none righteous, not even one" (Rom. 3:10b).

If repentance is taken out, there is no gospel left. There is no Good News until someone has admitted the bad news. The bad news is that we are sinners and responsible for our plight. We made the mess on Planet Earth. We are where we are because we rebelled against God and are lost. Only when we accept that judgment as genuine can we hear the good news that says God has acted in Christ to take away our sin and give us eternal life.

It is so easy to feel smug and secure. So let me play a little mind game with you based on Luke 13:1-5. Are you better than the people of India who are starving? Do you think the Bay Area earthquake was a punishment of God against Californians? Were the victims of the last airline crash you read about in the newspaper more sinful than the group you rode with on your last flight? Tragedies such as these are *not* divine judgments, yet each one reminds all of us of the uncertainty of life and calls us to live before God in an attitude of penitence. Acknowledging our need of him. Accepting grace.

Conclusion

Occasional stories of the brazenly impenitent send chills up our spines. Take the case of Theodore Streleski. When he was released from a California prison after serving seven years for beating a man to death, he was unable to say that he would not kill again. Reporting on his release, *Time* magazine called him "still unrepentant over the brutal murder" for which he had served time.

There are other stories of false or aborted repentance that sadden us. It made newspaper headlines a few years ago when Larry Flynt, the notorious pornographer, announced that he had become a born-again Christian. But in his next *Penthouse* editorial, he pledged that he would henceforth try to follow the spirit of Buddha and Christ. Most common, however, is the formalization of repentance into a brief ceremony without real transformation. A "step" prior to baptism. A prayer before the assembled church.

Repentance is a judgment against self as someone who deserves only hell. No claim against God. No way to make things right. Simply turning to God now to throw oneself on his mercy. Accepting through Christ what one can never have any other way.

Then, with real repentance having taken place, there can be rejoicing. A sense of relief. Celebration. With the prodigal son back at home, the Father can be happy.

For Reflection and Discussion

1. In what sense might one understand the word "happiness" in relation to God? How is it used in this chapter?

2. Review the first two parables of Luke 15. What is their common conclusion about the ending of the second? What does that say about God's attitude toward human repentance?

3. Document Luke's special interest in the theme of repentance. In what ways does he make explicit what is implicit in other Gospels?

4. What is the meaning of Jesus' teaching in Luke 13:1-5? Is all suffering a type of punishment for sin?

5. Name some behaviors we often confuse with repentance. Specify the difference between each of them and genuine repentance.

6. What insights into the nature of repentance come from the teaching of John the Baptist as recorded in this Gospel?

7. Trace the progressive steps of repentance that are modeled in the Parable of the Prodigal Son.

8. What is *restitution* as an element of repentance? How often is it possible to perform? Is it necessary when it is possible?

9. Reflect on the quotations from Tozer and Orr.

10. Why is repentance such a difficult thing for us? What feature of human personality is most offended by it?

Chapter 8

People Need Each Other

Sixty-four-year-old George Herbert Walker Bush took the oath of office as forty-first President of the United States on January 20, 1989. In his inaugural speech, he pledged to make his time as president the "Age of the Offered Hand." These sentences are from the text of his inauguration speech:

> My friends, we are not the sum of our possessions. They are not the measure of our lives. We cannot hope only to leave our children a bigger car, a bigger bank account. We must hope to give them a sense of what it means to be a loyal friend, a loving parent, a citizen who leaves his home, his neighborhood and town better than he found it.

The "offered hand" went out in the form of proposals for new beginnings with international friends and foes, bipartisan government at home, and improved race relations. History will record whether the dream becomes reality. But the speech affirmed that people really do need each other, that life is lived best in community.

Recent research published from the University of Michigan[1] affirms the need of people to reach out to one another, to end their social isolation, to establish close contact with one another. In a study of 37,000 persons in the United States, Finland, and Sweden, with some of the people followed over periods of up to 12 years, it was found that the lack of close social ties in and of itself significantly heightens susceptibility to illness and death. In a study of 2,754 men and women, isolated men were almost three

[1] "Researchers Adding the Sounds of Silence to the List of Health Risks," *New York Times*, 4 August 1988, p. 21.

times more likely to die at any age than men with close social ties. Men, in fact, were shown to be more devastated by isolation than women. This is probably true, the researchers said, because women tend to have a higher quality of relationships than men.

In the study in question, the category of "socially isolated" persons embraces the 10 to 20 percent of people who say they have nobody with whom to share their private feelings about life or who have close contact with others less than once per week. They are the people who believe that nobody cares enough about them to love them so unconditionally.

What President Bush suggested we set as a national agenda and what scientific studies tell us is important for human life is part of the ongoing agenda of the church. Jesus Christ is the Savior, not simply of the offered hand, but of the open arms. And his church is supposed to be a place of closeness and warmth by virtue of the Holy Spirit who fills each member of the body and collectively bonds us to one another.

We need to live in relationship with one another. I don't need the sense of being alone and isolated from you. You don't need to be a Lone Ranger Christian. When we retreat from one another, withdraw from one another, and shut one another out, life gets very lonely. And spirituality suffers.

To some degree or other, all of us are tempted to wear masks. I don't necessarily mean that people tend to be hypocritical. I'm not making that sort of judgment about people in general. Something much less sinister than hypocrisy is the issue here. It is the sense of fear that we all have about being very open with one another. It causes us to wear masks and deny certain feelings that we have. To pretend that things are other than they really are. And to keep other people at a distance when we're really hurting badly and need to let them into our lives.

Jesus has always offered himself as the Savior of the Open Arms and has intended for his church to be a place of close, social relationships in the Holy Spirit. As we continue to study Luke's special insights into Jesus that were turned into selling points for presenting him to the Roman world, we will focus on our need of one another as believers who live in community.

The Social Life of Jesus

Luke had significant insight into the personal life of Jesus which helped him understand what a community of faith called "the church" is supposed to be. Luke stressed that Jesus wanted us to see that we really do need each other.

Jesus was not a monk, a monastic, a hermit. In fact, one of the contrasts that people saw between John the Baptist and Jesus was that John tended to be very much of an isolationist. He tended to spend a lot of his time out in the desert alone. If John was ascetic and isolated, though, Jesus did not follow his pattern of personal behavior. The man from Nazareth was very much aware of the difference between him and his cousin John. He was also aware that others saw the difference and tried to use the lifestyle of each against himself. "For John the Baptist came neither eating bread nor drinking wine, and you say, 'He has a demon,' " said Jesus. "The Son of Man came eating and drinking, and you say, 'Here is a glutton and a drunkard, a friend of tax collectors and sinners' " (7:33-34).

It was H. J. Cadbury who first called attention to the many references in Luke's Gospel to inns, feasts, entertainment, and social life. There are three instances, for example, of Jesus' dining in the home of Pharisees at formal banquets. There is the famous one at the home of Simon where the woman came in, washed his feet with her tears, and dried them with her hair (7:36-50). Another one was

95

with an unnamed Pharisee (11:37-44), and still a third with a "prominent Pharisee," again left unnamed, on a Sabbath day (14:1-4).

Then there are some accounts of Jesus' social interaction in a variety of settings. Bethany, and the house of Mary, Martha, and Lazarus in particular, seems to have been something of a social hub for him. He seems to have been very fond of this family, and several episodes in the Gospels center on events growing out of their mutual friendship (cf. 10:38-42).

Luke also takes us along with Jesus into the house of Zacchaeus the publican. Zacchaeus invited some other people like himself, city outcasts and prostitutes, to dine with him and Jesus. Before the meal was over, such a rapport had been established between guest and host that the short, unpopular Zacchaeus was pouring out his heart to Jesus. Confessing some things about his life which needed to be laid before God. Making promises about restitution for tax bills he had overcharged certain people. Before the episode was finished, Jesus was able to say, "Today salvation has come to this house" (19:1-10).

Then there was Jesus' encounter with two travellers on the Emmaus Road. Jesus was walking down the same road as those two men and began to talk with them. Next thing you know, he invited himself to go in and eat with them. As he was breaking bread with them, he revealed himself to them (24:28-32).

The point of listing these social encounters at Bethany, in Zacchaeus' house, and on the Emmaus Road is simply that Jesus was an outgoing person. He didn't rent an office and wait for people to seek him out. He moved in the natural environment of his time, went to dinner parties, visited in the homes of friends, and struck up conversations with strangers. In the context of all this activity, he brought the presence of God into the lives of the people he met.

Going a step further, some of Jesus' best-known parables focus on community life. In those three famous parables in Luke 15 about the lost sheep, the lost coin, and the lost boy, recall how all three of them end. The shepherd, the woman, and the father called their neighbors together and had a celebration. The lost sheep was back in the fold. The lost coin had been found. The son who had been as good as dead was alive again. In all three cases, the parables end with parties being held to celebrate the happy endings which had come of such sad beginnings. The point seems clear. Life is best when shared with others.

Against the generally bad reputation of public inns from that time, Luke has Jesus' parents seeking lodging at an inn in Bethlehem on the night when he was born (2:7). In the story of the Good Samaritan, the Samaritan leaves the man at an inn in the care of a compassionate, sympathetic, honest inn-keeper (10:35). Luke did not understand Jesus to be an isolationist who was calling his church to disengage from all contact with the society in which it exists.

Finally, don't overlook the fact that Jesus compared the kingdom of heaven to a lavish banquet in which everyone can participate:

> When one of those at the table with him heard this, he said to Jesus, "Blessed is the man who will eat at the feast in the kingdom of God."
> Jesus replied: "A certain man was preparing a great banquet and invited many guests. At the time of the banquet he sent his servant to tell those who had been invited, 'Come, for everything is now ready.'
> "But they all alike began to make excuses. The first said, 'I have just bought a field, and I must go and see it. Please excuse me.'
> "Another said, 'I have just bought five yoke of oxen, and I'm on my way to try them out. Please excuse me.'
> "Still another said, 'I just got married, so I can't come.'

"The servant came back and reported this to his master. Then the owner of the house became angry and ordered his servant, 'Go out quickly into the streets and alleys of the town and bring in the poor, the crippled, the blind and the lame.'

" 'Sir,' the servant said, 'what you ordered has been done, but there is still room.'

"Then the master told his servant, 'Go out to the roads and country lanes and make them come in, so that my house will be full. I tell you, not one of those men who were invited will get a taste of my banquet.' " (14:15-24; cf. 13:29).

There you have it. Jesus said the kingdom of God is going to be a great banquet. It will have been spurned by some. Yet those who accept his invitation will be together in a great community of faith. They will celebrate the glory and righteousness of God. They will celebrate the grace which opened the door to such a feast. They will celebrate their companionship with one another.

The Family/People of God: Reality or Pipe-dream?

Living the Christian life successfully is not a matter of mastering rugged individualism. Salvation is a matter of finding yourself incorporated into the body of Christ. It doesn't matter whether you are a foot or hand or elbow or ear. God sets you in the body as it pleases him. But God sets everybody who is saved *in the body*. All who are saved by the blood of the Son of God have also been born into the family of God. But is this concept of being one body or a spiritual family a reality in your experience? Or is it still a pipe-dream?

To be a member of Christ's church is to be part of the continuous story of a covenant community. Beginning in the Old Testament with the call of Abraham, believers are asked to go on an adventurous journey. There will be unannounced and unanticipated twists and turns along the way, but it is in the nature of faith to keep walking toward a goal. But your journey is not made alone. Abraham traveled with his extended family. Israel traveled as a nation. You and I travel with the church.

The church needs great times of gathering, celebration, and affirmation. These times remind us that we are sharing a faith adventure with others and are not alone. This is why God requires the church to be together regularly as a great *congregation.* To remind one another of our heavenly citizenship. To eat a meal of remembrance. To refocus our hearts on the goal of our faith.

The key term describing what should happen when the whole church is together on the Lord's Day is "celebration." The story of the cross must be told again and again. We must be reminded that we are redeemed people. The vision of heaven must get clearer for us. Thus worship shouldn't be dry and boring. To the contrary, worship ought to be a time of celebration and joy. It ought to be something you look forward to. When you get there and participate in it, something should really happen. The fellowship of that body of people together under Christ should be meaningful. The church has come together to celebrate Christ, to re-dedicate itself to discipleship, and to affirm its social identity as a community of faith.

The church also needs small group-sharing, not as an alternative to congregational assemblies but as a supplement to them. Bible classes sometimes serve that function. The best Bible classes are the ones where there is warmth and openness. Not somebody droning away in lecture style because he likes the sound of his own voice, but a small group in which people are encouraged to share ideas, questions, and doubts.

Homes need to be opened. This may come about in the form of a small-group study, with perhaps a dozen or so people together. Some churches actively encourage and help arrange these study groups. On the other hand, it may be nothing so formal as a study session. It may just be the friendly sharing of one's apartment or house with others. Old-fashioned hospitality. Conscious effort of sharing life with others rather than isolating from them.

There is also great value in one-on-one times of sharing. Friendships can become so close in Christ that one can open his or her heart with a faithful confidant. Time can be spent in prayer. Sensitive matters can be thought through in the safety of confidentiality and concern. These close and enduring relationships are critical for the growth of faith.

Historically, the church has vacillated between concern for congregational assemblies with meaningful worship on the one hand and the encouragement of small-group and one-on-one relationships on the other. They have somehow been perceived to be mutually exclusive. But that is a terrible mistake. The church needs both. Each undergirds the other. Whatever is accomplished in the celebration and affirmation of the whole church in assembly needs to be reinforced in the smaller groups which form within the life of a healthy church.

We simply must rediscover what Luke saw as integral to Christian discipleship: *koinonia*. Fellowship. Community. A sense of belonging. We need to affirm family identity in Christ. Open heart and open hearth. Letting others see behind our masks. First Peter 4:8-11 seems to summarize quite well what the church is supposed to be in this regard:

> Above all, love each other deeply, because love covers over a multitude of sins. Offer hospitality to one another without grumbling. Each one should use whatever gift he has received to serve others, faithfully administering God's grace in its various forms. If anyone speaks, he should do it as one speaking the very words of God. If anyone serves, he should do it with the strength God provides, so that

100

in all things God may be praised through Jesus Christ. To him be the glory and the power for ever and ever. Amen.

Christians really do need each other. We've got to do something to get over this fear that some of us seem to have of one another. We must make one another partners in the spiritual adventure we have undertaken in Christ.

In his *The Great Divorce*, C. S. Lewis pictures hell as an ever-expanding city with a progressive number of empty streets. He even describes the process of how it happens. The people arriving in Lewis' hell are so quarrelsome that they pick fights with their neighbors within 24 hours of getting there. The run-ins are deemed unpleasant enough that within a week the newcomer decides to move. The next street over is usually empty, for everyone there has quarreled. If he moves to an inhabited street, the freshman is sure to have another argument soon and to move on.

The process continues. People get farther and farther apart. Before long they are thousands of miles from the bus stop where all the newcomers from Earth first arrive. Only by peering into a telescope can the latest arrivals see the lights of the occupied houses of grizzled old-timers who live millions of miles away, not only from the bus stop now but from each other as well.

Some people seem not to be able to wait. They appear determined to experience hell on Earth. Quarrelsome men. Defensive women. Frightened, lonely, and guilt-consumed people. People living in spiritual isolation from everyone else. Christ came to break down barriers. To unite people. To bring us together in his body. To put an end to hell on Earth as well as to rescue us from the hell to come.

Not everyone who is isolated from people is that way from being disagreeable. Some people see themselves as unattractive, socially inept, or otherwise undesirable. Others fear they will be used, put down, or abandoned if they open up to someone else. And some have a self-image that tags them "unimportant" or "unlovable." We humans can be very harsh with ourselves.

People who feel their isolation from other human beings may blame the world for its coldness and unfriendly makeup. In which case, they further isolate themselves by blaming and finger-pointing instead of doing something positive to break out of their loneliness.

Nobody can bring the detached 10 to 20 percent of a church, office, or world out of isolation and into the security of acceptance and love. The quarrelsome person has to lighten up. The frightened-of-closeness person has to push himself to get to know someone well enough to open up to that individual. The person who sees herself as unattractive or unlovable must try to find someone who will listen and give a candid reaction to the areas where she feels so inadequate.

And that guilt-laden person who has isolated himself because he feels so ashamed, so unworthy, and so wretched must come to terms with whatever is locked away in the darkest corners of his heart. It must be laid open in the light of truth before a holy God. It must be confessed to someone who is close enough to God's own heart that he or she will react to what is shared with compassion rather than anathemas. It must be covered and washed away by the blood of Christ.

You've tried to come out of hiding and into the light? Someone betrayed you? Hurt you and drove you farther underground? You must summon up the courage to reach out again. And again and again, if necessary.

Do you fear that someone may reach out to you? Choose you to trust? Open the dark recesses of a closed, frightened, or guilty heart to you? You don't have to be scholarly. Say something profound. Know how to fix what is hurting that person. There are professional resources to draw on if the problem is genuinely severe. In most instances, however, you only need to listen. Weep with those who weep. Share what you know about the joy and peace of forgiveness in Christ. Be Jesus' presence with that person to hear, care about, and accept a lonely person into your heart and life.

The goal of a church that wants to be faithful to Christ in this regard must be to have enough openness that nobody has to hide. Nobody has to live with the fear of rejection. Nobody has to wear masks. The church is not a group of people bonded together in perfection. It is a body which is saved by virtue of its relationship with the head, who is Christ. The body itself has some bruises. It sometimes limps along. Its imperfections show. But the living Christ continues to give grace and acceptance.

Conclusion

Newscaster Charles Osgood told the story of two ladies who lived in a convalescent center. Each had suffered an incapacitating stroke. One woman's stroke left her left side impaired, while the other's stroke damaged her right side. Both of these ladies were accomplished pianists but had given up hope of ever playing again.

It occurred to the director of that convalescent center to put those two ladies on the same piano bench in front of a single keyboard. She sat them down at a piano and encouraged them to play solo pieces together. It was awkward at first. But, over a period of days and even weeks, these two ladies, each of whom now was pulled out of her personal pain and into relationship with someone else similarly impaired, were entertaining everybody else in the convalescent center with their beautiful music.

That's something of how the church is supposed to be. We need each other. Where I am weak, you may be

strong. Where I am strong may be where you're weak.
Because we are in the family of God and members of the
one body of Christ, there comes to be a coordination and
harmony which teaches us that we really do need each
other.

Luke thought it was important for the people who
read his Gospel to realize that Jesus set about to create a
kingdom of people who could live together in community. It
seems important still for us to understand that same truth.

For Reflection and Discussion

1. Why is the concept of *community* so important to human
beings? What is some of the biblical evidence for the need of it?

2. What does Luke tell us about the social life of Jesus? Contrast
his social life with that of John the Baptist.

3. What do Jesus' parables recorded at Luke 15 tell us about a
sense of community and fellowship?

4. What significance do you attach to the fact that the kingdom
of God is compared to a great banquet in Luke 14?

5. In what sense is the church intended to be a "covenant
community" or the "family of God"? How do congregational, small-
group, and one-on-one settings relate to one another in church life?

6. What is the significance of the term *koinonia* when used of the
church?

7. Does 1 Peter 4:8-11 help you understand the meaning of
koinonia? Can you suggest another text that gives insight into the
concept?

8. What do you think of C. S. Lewis' metaphor in *The Great
Divorce*? What are some of the reasons which account for people
distancing themselves from one another?

9. What is the role of the church in nurturing spiritual health
among its members? How can you draw on the church for your spiritual
growth? How can you contribute to the nurturing of others?

10. What is the best illustration you have ever witnessed of the
church fulfilling its role as a *community of faith*?

Chapter 9

Everyone Must Choose

There are choices to be made in life, and some of those choices are anything but easy. Maybe you've heard a story that made the rounds a while back about how difficult some choices can be.

A woman had just gone through a terrible divorce experience. It had been a bitter, rancorous thing. Charge and counter charge. An unpleasant court encounter. But now it was over, and the divorce was final.

She had taken off a few days just to try to compose herself. Get her wits together. Set a course for her future. One day, as she was walking along the beach, she spied a bottle. She picked it up. Then, as she began dusting sand off it, out popped a genie. And the genie spoke to the woman. (You're already ahead of me with the "genie" business, aren't you?)

"You have three wishes to make," said the genie. "Whatever you ask will be done. However, I will tell you in advance that whatever is granted to you will also be given twice over to your former husband."

What a dilemma! She could have anything she wanted, but the man who had treated her so badly and from whom she had just been granted a divorce would get the same thing in double quantity. She was simultaneously elated at her own bright prospects and sickened that he would receive twice her own good fortune.

Trying hard to be realistic about her hard decisions, she thought of her need for a place to live. So she asked the genie for a three-bedroom, three-bathroom house on an acre lot. Poof! No sooner had she made her request than she was transported to the den of her new house. It was exactly what she had requested. Perfect in every detail. As she was looking around in child-like wonder, the genie took some wind from her sails by saying, "But remember, please, that your ex-husband was just transported to his new house which has six bedrooms, six baths, and a two-acre lot." She sat down dejectedly and put her head in her hands to think about her second wish.

Knowing that she would need money for her new life, she told the genie, "My second wish is to have a million dollars." Whoosh! In the instant she spoke the words, a million dollars in cash appeared on a table in the den of her beautiful new house. Running her fingers through the money to convince herself that it was real, she heard the genie say, "But remember that your former husband is running his fingers through two million dollars in cash on the table in his den." It was almost more than she could bear!

So she sat down to ponder her third and final request. What should this one be? What would she ask? What would be appropriate, given the knowledge that her ex-husband was going to get twice what she asked? Suddenly, her face lit up. He eyes were wide with excitement. She stood to her feet, faced the genie, and said, "Here is my third wish: I want you to scare me *half* to death!"

Decisions, decisions, and more decisions. Life is the accumulation of all the good and bad choices one makes. No, some decisions aren't easy. Thus we try to postpone them. Some of them wind up being made by default. But no one can avoid the responsibility of making decisions.

The Christian experience involves the most fundamental and radical of all decisions, *the decision to be a disciple of the Lord Jesus.* There are not two decisions -- to be a Christian and to be a disciple. To be a Christian is to be a disciple. "He who is not with me is against me," said Jesus, "and he who does not gather with me, scatters" (Luke 11:23). It is an all-or-nothing matter. The Christian's decision, then, is not *whether* to be a disciple but *what sort* of disciple to be. One can be faithful or unfaithful, with Christ or against him, gathering with him or scattering. Everyone who decides to accept salvation pledges simultaneously to be a faithful follower.

In this chapter, then, we turn to another matter of emphasis in Luke's Gospel. We focus on *discipleship*. As a Gentile physician interpreted the meaning of a Savior who had come as a Jew to save the whole world, he made it clear that one's choice to believe on Jesus would be a revolutionary commitment affecting every aspect of life. On Luke's view of the matter, following Christ not only involved receiving something but giving everything.

Luke's Emphasis on Discipleship

Earlier in this book, a chapter on repentance was included. No one can repent and stay the same, for repentance is a wholehearted change of heart and life. Thus, everything said in that lesson could be repeated here or regarded as preamble to this chapter. Repentance is at the very root of discipleship, and there is no discipleship without it. Once repentance begins, the person involved adopts a new perspective on life.

The things Luke stresses in his Gospel and Acts combine to spotlight the truth that nothing less than a new attitude toward life is adequate for a Christian. Commenting on Luke's use of "the Way" as a favorite way to designate Christianity, Leon Morris has said:

> It draws attention to Christianity as a whole way of life, not simply as a means of satisfying religious impulses. And Luke does not speak of "a" way, but "the" way; the expression points to a deep conviction of the rightness of Christianity and of the impossibility of any other way of leading people to God.[1]

[1]Leon Morris, *New Testament Theology* , p. 196.

Of course, the same truth of Christianity's exclusivity and its demand of singular loyalty is found in the other Gospels. There is no attempt here to say that Luke teaches something the other Synoptics and John do not. But it is unquestionably a point of special emphasis with Luke.

Even in the materials he shares with the other Synoptists, Luke has an emphatic way of telling certain things. He sometimes puts in emphatic details that the other writers omit or gives a literary twist to the telling of an event that effectively intensifies the story.

Take, for example, the call of the four fishermen to be disciples. Jesus called Peter, Andrew, James, and John by challenging them henceforth to be with him to "fish" for men. Both Matthew and Mark end the account with these words: "At once they *left their nets* and followed him" (Matt. 4:20; Mark 1:18). But Luke doesn't just say they left their nets and followed. Luke ends the account more emphatically by writing: "So they pulled their boats up on shore, *left everything* and followed him" (5:11).

Something very similar happens in the account of Matthew's being called to discipleship. Matthew, the tax collector, was sitting at his table receiving the taxes and entering amounts in his ledger books. Although the same story is told in the other Synoptic Gospels, Luke alone adds the detail that Matthew "left everything" and followed Jesus. It seems critical for Luke that his readers should understand what discipleship involves. When someone heeds the call to follow Jesus, he walks away from everything else to walk with him.

To what the other Gospel writers say about taking up one's cross and bearing it, Luke adds that the cross must be taken "daily" (9:23).

Matthew and Luke both tell of a series of encounters with would-be disciples. Jesus warned one man who had said he would follow him that the Son of Man, unlike even the foxes or birds, had no place to lay his head (9:57-58; cf. Matt. 8:19-20). Another said he would follow after first burying his father, and Jesus told him, "Let the dead bury their own dead" (9:59-60; cf. Matt. 8:21-22). Only Luke adds: "Still another said, 'I will follow you, Lord; but first let me go back and say good-by to my family.' Jesus replied, 'No one who puts his hand to the plow and looks back is fit for service in the kingdom of God' " (9:61-62). Luke understood discipleship to be a call for unreserved surrender to the claims of Christ. He was at great pains to underscore this important teaching.

Luke, along with Matthew, preserves a bold statement from Jesus about hating one's closest relatives for the sake of discipleship: "If anyone comes to me and does not hate his father and mother, his wife and children, his brothers and sisters -- yes, even his own life -- he cannot be my disciple" (14:25-27; cf. Matt. 10:37-38).

In Luke 14:28-33, there are two parables unique to Luke. Both parables make a similar point about counting the cost of discipleship. The first parable is about a farmer making a decision about building a tower. It is evidently some sort of addition or ornamentation to his house. Yet, observed Jesus, a man planning such a project does not begin without counting the cost involved. Otherwise he stands to be embarrassed by beginning a project and having to abandon it without being able to finish.

The second parable is about a king who gets word that another king is coming against him with 20,000 soldiers. So the king does some quick calculations. He only has 10,000 men. Are they better trained and better armed? Can he withstand the larger army with his troops? He counts the cost. If he decides that it is hopeless, he will send somebody to negotiate terms of peace before the advancing army arrives.

The two parables are similar but they make slightly different points. The builder of a tower is free to build or not as he chooses, but the king is being invaded (the other *comes against him*). He must do something. *Cf.* A. M. Hunter, 'In the first parable, Jesus said, "Sit down and reckon whether you can afford to follow me." In the second he says, "Sit down and reckon whether you can afford to refuse my demands."' Both ways of looking are important.[2]

Luke is always emphatic about discipleship. It is all or nothing. It is wholehearted commitment and will not bear halfhearted trifling. Discipleship is all day, every day; otherwise it is simply not discipleship.

What is Discipleship?

Discipleship is not easy to understand in our culture. On the one hand, many of us have been stroked, pacified, and pampered so long that we will not allow any demands to be made of us. If we think that anything is going to be expected of us, we run. On the other hand, there is the legalism which is practiced in the name of commitment and discipleship. Both of these are wrong-headed approaches to a subject Luke took seriously and thought the readers of his Gospel should understand as part of the meaning of Jesus.

In simplest possible terms, *discipleship is loving the things Jesus loved, wanting the things he wanted, and doing the things he did.*

Jesus loved the Father. He loved the words of the Father found in Scripture, and he loved communion with the Father in prayer. He wanted to experience his Father's presence, so he would spend times in solitude and meditation with him. That tells us something about discipleship expectations for us.

[2]Leon Morris, *The Gospel According to Luke* (Grand Rapids: William B. Eerdmans, 1974), p. 236.

Jesus loved righteousness because it gives glory to the Father. And he wanted the experience of the kingdom of God to become a reality among men and women on Earth. He prayed for it, and he tried to bring it about.

Jesus loved people made in the image of God, so he wanted the lost to be sought and found. So he went among the lost and spent more time with them than with the power brokers of the religious establishment. When he was criticized for failing to live up to establishment expectations, he talked about how the sick need a doctor worse than healthy people.

Jesus went where the hurting, the lonely, the hungry, and the sick were. He touched them. He fed them. He became involved in their lives. He allowed himself to be caught up in their pain and troubles. Whatever they were struggling with by virtue of their humanity, he was compelled to take to himself.

Discipleship to Jesus puts one in position to be doing the very same things he did. Loving the Father and seeking him in the Word, prayer, and meditation. Getting involved with the poor, sick, and lost. Occasionally running into conflict with people whose religious concerns are fixed, institutional, and traditional.

Discipleship also puts believers in situations where they will not be understood by people they are helping. A while back, I was involved briefly in helping a girl who was running from a Satanic cult. She had been a cult member for four and a half years, but now she was frightened for her life and running from it. She described the initiation she had been put through when she joined the cult. It was an evil and repulsive ceremony. She described the life she had lived with the group over the past four years. She and several other girls had been prostituted by the cult over that period of time to bring money in to support the group. She had had three abortions and several bouts with venereal disease. All the alcohol she had drunk in order to sleep at night had begun to take its toll on her liver.

A friend and I spent time trying to make her feel safe, for the group had made death threats against anyone who ever left. We explored shelter possibilities. Checked with police authorities about her safety. Looked into a place for alcohol detoxification and job training. All the while, we were trying to point her in the direction of a new spiritual orientation for her life.

The more we learned about her, the more our hearts ached for her. She contacted and eventually joined the Satan cult because of what she was running from at home. For three and one-half years before she ran away, her father had been abusing her sexually. For two years before she ran away, he had been selling her to other men. Still in her teens, here was a girl who had never had a break. And we were determined to do anything within our power to treat her as we believed Jesus would. To be his disciples. To be her chance for something different.

Then, right in the middle of some discussions about options she could take and choose among, her head snapped up. She looked me straight in the eyes and said, with a tone that sounded accusing, "Why are you doing this?" As I tried to make sense of her tone, my mind raced over what I had learned about her. She didn't know anything about Jesus. She had no frame of reference for understanding somebody doing something for her without any strings attached. Then I thought of a way to answer her question in light of her background. I said, "You've done what you've done for the last several years because you have been a follower of Satan, right?"

"Yes," she said.

"You and I both see what that has done to you. Satan has let people hurt you and use you and exploit you. But I am a follower of Jesus of Nazareth, and he doesn't hurt people or use them or exploit them. It is his way to care about people, help them, and ask nothing for himself. I'm just trying to do what I think Jesus would do if he were sitting in this room with you right now."

Then I deliberately added one more statement to provoke a conversation I thought we needed to have. I said, "I'm doing it because I love you."

A tiny smile came across her face, probably best described as a smirk, and she said, "Oh, you want sex."

"Not on your life," I answered. "But I used the word 'love' because I figured that was probably what it meant to you."

"My leader says that love means having sex with somebody," she said.

"I would expect him to tell you that, but my leader is Jesus and he says that loving people is caring about them and trying to do what is good for them and not ever using or hurting them in the process."

"I don't understand that."

"I know you don't. All I can do is ask that you let us try to do some things to help you and teach you that the word 'love' can mean something other than what you've been told it means."

I wish I knew how her story is going to end. I just know that it illustrates two very different leaders and two very different types of discipleship.

Dietrich Bonhoeffer's oft-quoted statement about discipleship is this: "When Christ calls a man he bids him come and die." And that was Luke's point as well. Discipleship is leaving everything that stands between you and Jesus. It is making a costly decision. It is valuing the gospel for what it is.

Cheap grace is grace without discipleship, grace without the cross, grace without Jesus Christ, living and incarnate.

Costly grace is the gospel which must be *sought* again and again, the gift which must be *asked* for, the door at which a man must *knock*.

Such grace is *costly* because it calls us to follow, and it is *grace* because it calls us to follow *Jesus Christ*. It is costly because it costs a man his life, and it is grace because it gives a man the only true life. It is costly because it condemns sin, and grace because it justifies the sinner. Above all, it is *costly* because it cost God the life of his Son: "ye were bought at a price," and what has cost God much cannot be cheap for us. Above all, it is *grace* because God did not reckon his Son too dear a price to pay for our life, but delivered him up for us.[3]

An Imaginary Conversation

One day a believer came before Jesus to talk with his Savior and Master. He said, "Lord Jesus, there are some matters we've needed to sort out for a long time. It keeps nagging at me that we are probably working at opposite purposes, so perhaps we need to talk. Clear the air. Lay all our cards on the table.

"Jesus, I love you but have to seek my own fulfillment rather than your kingdom when the two are in conflict. It's just human nature. After all, you made me the way I am.

"I love you, Jesus, but must hold to my friends, even the ones who cannot bring me closer to you and who often tempt me to sin against you. You surely understand about my need to be accepted by my peers.

"You know, Jesus, that I love you with my whole heart. But I can't think you want me to sacrifice my money, my comfort, or my prestige, even though they are most often for my glory than for yours.

"Jesus, I really do love you but sometimes have this overwhelming urge to get even with people who hurt me

[3]Dietrich Bonhoeffer, *The Cost of Discipleship*, rev. ed., trans. R. H. Fuller (New York: The Macmillan Co., 1963), pp. 47-48.

114

rather than turn the other cheek to them. It just doesn't seem fair to have to take that stuff from anybody.

"Lord, you know I love you. But my self-esteem gets such a boost from leading and dominating that I just can't feel right being a follower and a servant. After all, what would my colleagues think of me in such a self-effacing role? It just wouldn't be me.

"Jesus, I love you but am having a difficult time with several of my neighbors, even my Christian brothers and sisters. Some of them are rude and selfish. Others are hypocritical. Why, I have to wonder whether some of them even love you very much at all.

"This little talk we've had has made me feel a lot better. I think we probably understand each other better now. Do you have anything to say?"

Jesus' eyes looked as sad as they ever have at that moment. As they filled with tears, he said, "You've said all there is to say. Your position is clear. There's nothing I can add."

The two then went their separate ways. One walked away with a jaunty spring in his step. The other walked away slowly, as if he were carrying the weight of the world on his back.

Their paths never crossed again.

Conclusion

The Jesus Christ that Luke had come to know still calls men and women to be his disciples. Luke's written Gospel and our own faithful proclamation of Jesus still challenge people to a moment of encounter with him.

Beethoven's *Fifth Symphony in C Minor* is built around a single musical phrase. A phrase of only four notes, it is memorable and stays with anyone who hears it. It is one short note repeated three times, followed by a longer note lower down the scale. If you don't know Beethoven but remember the Vanquish headache tablet commercials of a few years back, you know the phrase.

A tradition has it that Beethoven himself explained this haunting phrase to mean "Thus fate knocks at the door." Christians believe that it is Christ, not fate, who knocks at every heart's door. He confronts and calls us. He wants us to follow him and accept his call to discipleship.

For Reflection and Discussion

1. Define the words *disciple* and *discipleship* in your own words.

2. What is the relationship between choosing to be a Christian and making a commitment to discipleship? What is the real choice involved in a Christian's discipleship?

3. Review some of the events found in other Gospels that Luke tells with special emphasis in order to stress the implications of discipleship.

4. Study the statements on discipleship quoted from Jesus in Luke 9. What is unique to Luke's Gospel in relating this series of encounters?

5. Read the two parables in Luke 14:28-33. Have you ever thought about the distinction between them which is pointed out in the quotation from Morris?

6. What do you think of the definition of *discipleship* offered in this chapter? What implications does it have for your attitudes and behavior?

7. React to the Bonhoeffer distinction between "cheap grace" and "costly grace." Do you agree with his thesis? Can you illustrate the principle involved in it from your own experience?

8. What New Testament metaphor of discipleship do you find most impressive? Why?

9. This chapter contains a hypothetical conversation between a modern "disciple" and Jesus. Is anything in it believable? Does any part of it convict you?

10. What commitments or rededications do you feel compelled to make in light of this chapter?

Chapter 10

Knowing God's Will

How does one know that he or she is living within the will of God? We pray for God's will to be done. We affirm to one another that we want to do God's will. We say that someone is defying the will of God. What do we mean in using such a term?

I will frankly admit to being skeptical of the person who claims a pipeline to God or who affirms certainty about a divine blueprint for all his life. Yet I am equally skeptical of the person who has no sensitivity about seeking the will of God and who has no place for such a notion in his vocabulary.

Maybe you've heard the story of the naive fellow who believed he could find the will of God by setting his Bible on its spine, letting it fall open, and reading the first verse that caught his eye. He used that method to determine what he should do with some investments.

He got his Bible and let it fall open before him. It opened to Matthew 9, and his eyes landed on verse 37: "The harvest is plentiful but the workers are few." He took that to be a sign from God that he should invest in wheat futures. He did. And he lost thousands of dollars. Trying to rebound from his losses, he took out his Bible and again followed his established procedure for seeking God's will. This time it fell open at Mark 5, and his eyes came to rest on verse 11: "A large herd of pigs was feeding on the nearby hillside." He took it as a sign that he should invest in pork bellies. So he did, and lost the rest of his money.

Trying to figure out the meaning of the year's financial disaster, he decided to go back to the Word of God to seek still another sign. He opened his Bible one more time, and it fell open to the Gospel of Luke, *chapter 11*. So he called his lawyer and filed for bankruptcy.

The story illustrates how ridiculous it is to think that the will of God is such a random, haphazard thing which can be discovered by chance. If the will of God is blind luck and superstition, then the pagan's method of reading animal bones or horoscopes is just as good as the Christian method.

Is there a way by which people can know the will of God? Is there a means by which we can feel secure that we are living within the divine will? Is there a way by which we can live our lives with spiritual confidence?

Seeking Divine Direction

Surely it is the desire of every Christian to have a knowledge of God's will. Think about it for a minute: If you could have five minutes alone with God, what would you discuss?

Living the will of God would allow us to follow the example of Jesus and to have the confidence about our lives that he had about his. "I have brought you glory on earth by completing the work you gave me to do," he said to his Father (John 17:4). Furthermore, it would allow us to evaluate our lives from God's perspective and to live in confident hope. We would be able to say with Paul: "I have fought the good fight, I have finished the race, I have kept the faith. Now there is in store for me the crown of righteousness, which the Lord, the righteous Judge, will award to me on that day . . ." (2 Tim. 4:7-8).

Some people appear to think that only Jesus, Paul, and a few other notable figures of Bible history could make such confident assertions about God's will. On their view of the matter, it would be sheer presumption for anyone today to speak with such conviction as they did about knowing and doing the will of God.

Many of us would confess that we want that sort of confidence in our spiritual lives. From reading the Gospel of Luke, one gets the idea that Luke was interested in the same thing.

As this Gentile physician studied and interpreted the life of the Jewish Messiah, he saw a plan of God being worked out in his life. Yet it also seems clear that he saw Jesus as free and uncoerced. That is, he saw Jesus participating in the divine will by choice rather than by force. For example, the agonizing prayer in Gethsemane clearly assumed a divine plan for his actions yet also presumed that he had the freedom to refuse it. Thus the prayer: "Father, if you are willing, take this cup from me; yet not my will, but yours be done" (Luke 22:42).

The Father willed. The Son submitted. In this pattern is found the basis for confidence. It is possible, though, for us to turn our backs on God's will and to follow our own self-willed ways. In this pattern is found the path to spiritual failure.

Both in his Gospel and Acts, Luke expressed a fixed confidence that God has a plan for human history and that nothing can interfere with that plan being realized in the end. His further assumption was that each individual must bring his life into submission to that plan -- not that God will adjust it based on our whims. Whether our lives will count for anything within the divine plan involves choice on our part. Whether we find and live our places within that plan depends on conscious acts of seeking God's will.

Luke was not deterministic (i.e., what will be will be) in his view of history, and he never portrayed God as coercing people against their free wills. Neither did he ever represent God as dictating the particulars of each human life. God has a great Master Plan, and each of us is allowed the freedom to participate in that project or to reject involvement with it.

119

Luke's Concept of Divine Purpose

In the Gospel of Luke, there is a tremendous emphasis on God's will being allowed to unfold and develop among men. The Third Gospel is an account of things "fulfilled" among us (1:1).

God's purpose traces to eternity and was announced before man was driven from Eden. God's purpose, in a nutshell, is to crush the works of Satan beneath his feet and to see to it that the fallen race is brought to redemption through his Son. Satan must be defeated, and his head must be crushed (cf. Gen. 3:15b); redemption of sinful man must take place, even though a high price will have to be paid in the process.

That same unilateral purpose of God was repeated in connection with the promises made to Abraham. Not only did the Lord promise that Abraham's descendants would be "as numerous as the stars in the sky and as the sand on the seashore" and that they would "take possession of the cities of their enemies," but he also pledged that "through your offspring all nations on earth will be blessed" (Gen. 22:18).

The redemptive purpose of God has never been subject to alteration. Whether men cooperated or willed it to be so, God brought the Messiah and Redeemer at his appointed time. And his work of making salvation known to humanity is still unfolding in the world, no matter whether we foster that work or resist it. Heaven's goal of bringing many sons to glory is a fixed purpose. Within that resolute intention, all the events of our lives are to find their meaning. Whatever contributes to God's purpose is holy; all that opposes it is evil.

In the Gospel of Luke, Jesus is the perfect model of one who knows and pursues the divine will. He lives within Luke's narrative under divine sovereignty. From his childhood sense of heaven's rule over his actions to his consciousness as an adult that his death was within his Father's plan, Luke shows Jesus ordering all his decisions and actions according to God's plan.

Out of his Greek background, Luke knew a word which expressed the character of necessity or compulsion in an event. That Greek term (*dei* = it is necessary) appears 18 times in his Gospel. It conveys to us that Luke saw Jesus being compelled by a sense of loyalty to the will of God. Some things simply had to happen because they were consistent with God's will for his life. A few examples will help make this point about his life clearer.

When he was only 12, Jesus was lost briefly from his family after a trip to Jerusalem. When found in the temple courts discussing the Word of God with the teachers there, he answered Mary's scolding concern with an appeal to his sense of divine purpose. "Didn't you know *I had to be* in my Father's house?" he asked (2:49b).

When explaining why he had to move around in preaching rather than stay in one location, he appealed to this same sense of necessity. "I *must* preach the good news of the kingdom of God to the other towns also," he said, "because that is why I was sent" (4:43).

Once when Jesus healed a woman on the Sabbath, he was confronted by a synogogue ruler who was eager to enforce what he understood the Law of Moses to require. Jesus responded by appealing to a greater necessity within the divine will he knew from the Father. If we translate quite literally, the ruler protested, "There are six days on which it is necessary (Gk, *dei*) to work." Jesus answered, "Was it not necessary (Gk, *dei*) that this one be loosed from [Satan's] bond on the Sabbath day?" (13:14, 16). Compassion has a "necessity" within the divine will which is greater than that of legalistic interpretation.

In recording Jesus' affirmations in advance about the nature of his suffering and death, Luke used the vocabulary word for events with a necessary character several times. The *dei*-character of Christ's passion is affirmed at 9:22 ("The Son of Man *must* suffer many things and be rejected by the elders, chief priests and teachers of the law, and he *must* be killed and on the third day be raised to life", 17:25 ("But first he *must* suffer many things and be rejected by this generation"), 24:7 ("The Son of Man *must* be delivered into the hands of sinful men, be crucified and on the third day be raised again"), 24:26 ("*Did* not the Christ *have to* suffer these things and then enter his glory?"), and 24:44 ("Everything *must be* fulfilled that is written about me in the Law of Moses, the Prophets and the Psalms").

Writing about Luke's use of *dei*, one New Testament scholar observed:

> Jesus sees His whole life and activity and passion under this will of God comprehended in a *dei*. . . . It has its basis in the will of God concerning Him which is laid down in Scripture and which He unconditionally follows (Lk. 22:37; 24:44). His disciples, apostles and community are also laid under this *dei* which derives from the will of God. Claimed by the divine will, they are shaped and determined by it down to the smallest details of their lives (Lk. 12:12; Ac. 9:6, 16; 14:22; 19:21; 23:11; 27:24). . . . This will of God claims man in every situation of life and gives goal and direction to life on the basis of its saving purpose.[1]

Luke is also conscious of people who resist the purpose of God. "But the Pharisees and experts in the law rejected God's purpose for themselves, because they had not been baptized by John" (7:30).

God does have a plan for human history. God does have a purpose for holiness in individual lives. Jesus personifies how a life is lived within both God's broader purpose for history and his personal plan for individual holiness. Luke's goal in presenting his idea so compellingly

[1]*Theological Dictionary of the New Testament*, 1964 ed., s.v. *"dei, deon esti,"* by Grundmann.

in his Gospel seems clear. He wanted his readers to understand that God's will is to be done in this world and to fit our lives within that will.

In Luke's Gospel, then, there is an element of necessity about service to God by believers. Prayer, for example, is a necessity (18:1). So is speaking boldly for the Lord (12:12; cf. Acts 5:29). Christian service is not an option, and every Christian, from president to pauper, needs to understand that some things are essential to our lives by virtue of the divine will.

How to Know the Divine Will

How can you know the will of God for your life?

For one thing, you must understand the nature of the will you are seeking. The Bible doesn't teach that the will of God is some sort of blueprint or package of predetermined details for all the events of your life. To the contrary, God will unfold his purposes for you in the daily outworking of your commitment to him. Your greatest need is to cultivate a prayerful sensitivity to the presence and activity of God in daily events.

Paul wrote of this sort of surrender when he said of Christians: "We are God's workmanship, created in Christ Jesus to do good works" (Eph. 2:10a). It is his New Testament parallel to this familiar exhortation: "Trust in the Lord with all your heart and lean not on your own understanding; in all your ways acknowledge him, and he will make your paths straight" (Prov. 3:5-6).

It is also important to realize that the outworking of that commitment is done against the backdrop of God's general will which has been shown to all of us in Scripture. Everything that we are seeking for God to do in working out his *particular will* for our separate lives is going to happen within the framework of his *general will* for all men and women which is found in the Bible.

Most of us have watched sadly as people have used the tag "God's will" to package an excuse for walking against the revealed Word of God. I know of a man who had problems in his marriage. He had a series of several affairs, after each of which his wife took him back and tried to make the marriage work. He then met still another woman and initiated an affair, filed to divorce his wife, and announced his intention to marry his latest lover. He announced that all of this was "God's will," for he knew that God had willed his happiness. God does not reveal his will for the happiness of particular individuals by calling them to do things which expressly violate his revealed will about promise keeping and marital fidelity.

First, follow a spiritual path to discernment. Look first to the revealed and written Word of God for a command or a theological principle which relates to the matter at hand. If you find that, accept it as God's will and commit yourself to obeying it.

Second, assuming now that there is no explicit statement in Scripture about the matter in question, pray for divine wisdom to apply what you do know of God's general will to the issue at hand (Jas. 1:5).

Third, obey everything that you understand of God's will related to your situation. Do as much of what you know to be the *right* thing, even when you cannot see a guaranteed "happy ending" ahead.

Fourth, trust God to guide you through circumstances which he brings to bear in his providence.

Fifth, seek God's guidance through the counsel of older, more mature believers. In particular, seek out Christians who have had to deal with situations similar to your own and who have had more experience in seeking and doing the will of God in difficult times.

Finally, accept the freedom given you in Christ to make decisions in nonmoral areas, and do not hold God up to ridicule by assigning those decisions to him. Do you really think God cares what color dress you wear to church? Or whether you have waffles or eggs for breakfast? Yet some people attribute such things to him. God guides us in those things that are *real* decisions that affect the direction of our spiritual lives.

Conclusion

God does not guide us like dumb animals, pulling bits in our mouths by visions, dreams, or subjective prods, but by the exercise of our understanding. Growing daily into the likeness of our Lord Jesus, our minds are renewed and transformed; thus we gain experience and skill in being "able to test and approve what God's will is -- his good, pleasing and perfect will" (Rom 12:1-2). Our very thought patterns become more spiritual and produce more insightful decisions which give God glory.

Luke interpreted the life of Jesus as one of clear-headed direction and purpose within God's will. He also saw the possibility for himself and other disciples to follow the example of Jesus in living resolutely within God's purpose for mankind. Thus he wrote to show us a perfect example and to challenge us to walk the secure path of divine guidance.

Unlike the poor fellow described at the start of this chapter, God's direction does not come through some desperate procedure of allowing a Bible to fall open where it will. It comes with ever-increasing clarity to those who seek the Lord daily and who live before him with an attitude of responsive obedience.

For Reflection and Discussion

1. In your opinion, what does the expression "the will of God" mean to most people? How do they try to discover God's will?

2. What is *determinism*? Does the Gospel of Luke present a deterministic view of the will of God?

3. What does the Bible identify as God's purpose in relation to humankind? How was that purpose expressed in Eden? To Abraham?

4. In what sense is the purpose identified in question 3 unalterable and predestined? In what sense does it depend on human freedom?

5. The Greek word *dei* is important in Luke. What does it mean? What is its significance to the theme of this chapter?

6. Review the *dei*-passages listed in this chapter. How do you interpret the significance of the word in each case?

7. What is the relationship between what this chapter calls God's *general will* and his *particular will*?

8. What is your reaction to the six suggestions about discerning the will of God offered in this chapter?

9. What revisions would you suggest for making the six suggestions about knowing the will of God more helpful?

10. Is there a particular matter about which you need to discover the will of God today? Why not try the method offered in this chapter?

Chapter 11

How Goes the War?

War? What war?

Some people may not even know one is being fought. May not be aware that there in a conflict between the forces of light and the forces of darkness that encompasses this whole universe. That God and Satan are locked in a to-the-death struggle. That this war has really been going on since before the world was created. Or that all of us have some decisions to make about where we stand in it.

A recurring theme in Scripture is that a great battle is going on between the saints of God and the allies of Satan. From Eden forward, the conflict has been focused. Satan caused all of the race to fall by causing the original representatives of humanity to sin. While the guilt of what they did is not transmitted from generation to generation, the consequences of what they did still linger. The world is different from what it would have been if they had not sinned. Our environment is different. Our health is different. We have more and larger cemeteries than we would have ever needed if it hadn't been for the sin of that original pair.

In the New Testament epistles, Paul developed this theme in some detail. He insisted that Christians who are going to do battle with the enemy put on the full armor of God (cf. Eph. 6:10-18) He even traced the Christian armor from helmet to sandals and indicated the meaning of each part of his metaphor. Our helmet is salvation, and our feet are fitted with gospel readiness. There is a breastplate of righteousness, a shield of faith, and a belt of truth. In our hands is placed the sword of the Spirit, which is the Word of God.

Perhaps the most significant verse in that entire text is this: "For our struggle is not against flesh and blood, but against the rulers, against the authorities, against the powers of this dark world and against the spiritual forces of evil in the heavenly realms" (Eph. 6:12). From Paul's point of view on human life, everything had meaning in terms of its spiritual significance. He saw every event in his life in terms of a great conflict with eternal implications.

It is to our discredit that we seldom interpret what is going on in our experience in terms of *spiritual* conflict. When we read newspaper accounts of drug trafficking, we tend to explain it in terms of economics. When we see evening news reports of child abuse or political scandal, our conversations generally point to psychological accounts of what makes people act as we do. The prophets, evangelists, and writers of the early church saw things in a different light.

> After this the Lord appointed seventy-two others and sent them two by two ahead of him to every town and place where he was about to go. He told them, "The harvest is plentiful, but the workers are few. Ask the Lord of the harvest, therefore, to send out workers into his harvest field. Go! *I am sending you out like lambs among wolves. . . ."* (10:1-3).

As Jesus and his earliest followers interpreted their world, they did so in terms of conflict. Struggle. *War.*

Good and Evil in the Gospel of Luke

All through his Gospel, Luke underscores the conflict between good and evil in a variety of settings. He does not use Paul's metaphor of the Christian as a footsoldier. Yet he and Paul understood life in the same basic terms. A cosmic conflict is going on, and the destiny of human souls is at stake.

The Bible says that Satan is our enemy. He is always in combat with the people of God. Satan, his host of demons, and evil men under his power are at work to destroy the work of God in the world.

In spite of the fact that his personal fate has been sealed millennia ago, he has not given up the battle. Though he knows that he is damned beyond any hope of personal victory over our God, he is thrashing about in his death agony and trying to snare as many others in his dark fate as possible. He has powerful weapons to use against us, and we would be foolish to underestimate his cunning or determination. All this does not mean, however, that we are hopeless before his intrigues.

In Luke's account of Jesus, the war raging between good and evil focuses on the *demons* and *evil men* who have set themselves against the Son of God. The decisive event which appears to bring the struggle to its climax is the *cross*. Yet it is the *resurrection* which demonstrates who will have the ultimate victory.

Taking on Christ's Cause

With nothing more than a casual reading of the Gospel of Luke, there can be no doubt that Jesus is always in competition with evil. In the wilderness temptation (4:1-13), there was no doubt about Satan's intention. His goal was to seduce the Son of God into sin and to destroy him by alienating him from his Father. And if, as 1 Corinthians 10:13 appears to teach, there is a direct link between temptation and the power to endure, the intensity of Jesus' temptations in the wilderness must have been beyond our ability to imagine.

Whenever Jesus was in personal battle with Satan during his ministry, he was always decisively victorious over him. Satan, knowing that there was more than one way to hurt Jesus and to frustrate his work, did not always confront him so directly as in the wilderness. He sometimes focused his attacks on the disciples and would-be disciples of Jesus rather than on him personally.

When he taught publicly, Jesus acknowledged that Satan was contending with him for souls. He also admitted that Satan's successes were intrusions into his plan for bringing all men and women to the Father. In his famous Parable of the Soils (8:4-15), Jesus began by speaking of some of the farmer's seed which fell along the path only to be walked on and eaten by birds. This element of the parable was explained by him this way: "Those along the path are the ones who hear, and then the devil comes and takes away the word from their hearts, so that they may not believe and be saved."

It becomes clear in a statement such as this that the struggle is not just between Jesus and the devil. Everyone who becomes a disciple of Jesus has entered the spiritual warfare for God which obligates him to wrestle against the devil.

In Luke's Gospel, a considerable portion of the struggle focuses on the demons. Demon possession is scarcely mentioned in Scripture except in the Synoptics. It was a terrible thing which could take place even against the person's will. Innocent children, good people, covenant people -- all could be taken captive. They could be possessed against their wills and be hurt physically. Made to do bizarre things. Used for the most wicked of purposes.

On a variety of occasions, Jesus showed that his power was greater than Satan's. Whenever he encountered one or more of these evil spirits, he would show that he had power over them. He would cast them out. He would break their power.

When Jesus sent the disciples out on their first preaching tour, he warned them plainly about the spiritual contest they were entering. As they preached, they met the same sort of demonic opposition Jesus encountered personally. When they returned and reported to him on their work, one of the things that impressed them most was that they were able to overcome those dark powers. "The seventy-two returned with joy and said, 'Lord, even the demons submit to us in your name' " (Luke 10:17). His response to them is interesting: "He replied, 'I saw Satan fall like lightning from heaven' " (Luke 10:18). This episode and response proves that Satan is defeated whenever Christ's disciples experience spiritual success.

An important text about spiritual conflict in the Gospel of Luke focuses on a man who was unable to speak because of demon possession. Luke writes:

> Jesus was driving out a demon that was mute. When the demon left, the man who had been mute spoke, and the crowd was amazed. But some of them said, "By Beelzebub, the prince of demons, he is driving out demons." Others tested him by asking for a sign from heaven (11:14-15).

An interesting thing about the miracles of Jesus is that even his bitterest enemies never denied that he was doing mighty works and miracles. But the expulsion of the demon in this case caused some of those enemies to attribute his miracle-working power to Beelzebub. Notice Jesus' reply to such an idea:

> Jesus knew their thoughts and said to them: "Any kingdom divided against itself will be ruined, and a house divided against itself will fall. If Satan is divided against himself, how can his kingdom stand? I say this because you claim that I drive out demons by Beelzebub. Now if I drive out demons by Beelzebub, by whom do your followers drive them out? So then, they will be your judges. But if I drive out demons by the finger of God, then the kingdom of God has come to you" (11:17-20).

131

Jesus challenged his critics to examine his deeds in light of their own theology about demons. Mind you, he did not admit that their theories or ceremonies were valid; he simply based his reply on what he knew they believed. The Pharisees, for example, believed in the reality of demon possession. They even had some ceremonies of exorcism that they would go through on behalf of someone they deemed possessed by Satan. For myself, I doubt that their rituals had any real power. For the sake of his argument, however, that is beside the point.

Jesus' argument was basically this: "If you condemn me, then you condemn yourselves! If the ability to cast out demons means that the one doing it is in league with the prince of the devils, then your followers who cast out demons must also be partnered with him!" It was a pretty shrewd approach, don't you think? They had to either back away from their condemnation of him or broaden their harsh judgment to their own disciples.

With his detractors on the defensive, he pressed the divided-kingdom argument. Any kingdom or common-wealth whose rulers are fighting among themselves is setting itself up to collapse. If Beelzebub, the prince of the demons, was using his power through Jesus to cast out demons, then he is through. Far from proving that Jesus was in league with Satan, then, his ability to cast out demons proved that the Kingdom of God had broken into human experience.

The story isn't over just yet. On the heels of this confrontation and the devastation of his enemies, he gave another parable. Its application is far wider than the immediate confrontation which was at hand that day. Its point strikes home to us as powerfully as to its original hearers.

When a strong man, fully armed, guards his own house, his possessions are safe. But when

132

someone stronger attacks and overpowers him, he takes away the armor in which the man trusted and divides up the spoils. He who is not with me is against me, and he who does not gather with me, scatters" (11:21-23).

We must choose sides! *There is no neutrality here.* There is a war going on. It is between Christ and Satan. The fact that Jesus has proved himself stronger than Satan (by casting out demons and, eventually, by rising from the dead) proves that the Kingdom of God has arrived. So the time has come for each of us to choose where he or she will stand. Everyone must take sides. What is going on is too everlastingly important for anyone to feign indifference.

As the Gospel of Luke continues, more events are explained in terms of the great antagonism between good and evil. Moving to the book's climax, Satan is credited with being behind Judas' act of betrayal (22:3). Furthermore, Satan was determined to sift Peter as wheat (22:31).

With the battle at its peak and with the decisive contest at hand, the cross became the critical focus as to the final outcome of the contest. In the early stages of arrest, trial, and crucifixion, Satan appeared on his way to victory. "But this is your hour," said Jesus to the men come to arrest him, "when darkness reigns" (22:53b). In the resurrection, however, the tables were turned. Satan was decisively and eternally defeated.

The Conflict Continues

"But if Satan has been 'decisively and eternally defeated,' why is life so hard for people who want to do right?" asks someone.

Human life is still lived in the arena of cosmic conflict. Light and dark. Life and death. God and Satan. There has still been no peace accord struck between these opposing forces. The Berlin Wall may have been breached, but the dividing wall between the Kingdom of God and the domain of evil is fixed and steadfast.

You and I can no more be neutral in our generation than the Pharisees could be in theirs. You're on one side or the other. If you insist on trying to be neutral, you automatically fall into the camp of the enemy. If you are not on Jesus' side, you are against him. If you are not gathering with Jesus into the Kingdom of God, then you are scattering his sheep and fighting his purpose of uniting them under his care.

Murderers, child pornographers, drug traffickers, and people who ensnare the poor in things ranging from gambling to stealing to prostitution are all pawns of Satan. To the degree that any one of us walks into his traps or consciously pursues evil, we become either victims of or collaborators with Satan.

Our struggles focus on three concerns.

The first is what the Bible calls our *sinful nature*. By this term ("flesh," KJV) a lifestyle of self-centered behavior is meant. It refers to the habits we have developed by virtue of yielding to temptation and listening to Satan's lies. Pride, selfishness, and sensuality (cf. 1 John 2:15-17) are at the heart of the sinful nature. We can see how self-destructive this lifestyle is. But what are we to do? Can a self-help manual guide us to victory?

The second issue we face is our *insufficiencies*. Life takes us to our limits, reduces us to tears, and impresses us with our inadequacy to cope. All of us are stretched at times beyond any resources that we have, and we can collapse in those situations. Sometimes we pretend, lie, and fake competency. We smile and say that everything is all right, when we know good and well that it isn't.

Third, there are *uncertainties about the future*. Unable to control today and insufficient for what is challenging us, we are anxious about the unknown future. Even if we "secure our future" in terms of economics, we still face

134

death. We all know we're going to die. The human race has lived in terror of death from the beginning. How do we deal with our uncertainties about the future?

The War is Already Won!

Does this talk of war, demons, and ongoing conflict sound threatening to you? Does thinking about your personal spiritual struggles dishearten you? The goal of this chapter has no such negative tone to it.

Go back to Luke 10:20 for the good news which puts everything else in clearer perspective. How goes the war? *The war has already been won!* Some days may not reflect victory. We may still have personal setbacks and disappointments. But, for all practical purposes, the truth of the matter is that the war is over. "Do not rejoice that the spirits submit to you," said Jesus as his disciples returned from their first preaching campaign, "but rejoice that your names are written in heaven" (10:20).

Most of us know the old caution saying about "winning the battle and losing the war." Christians need to learn that, while we will occasionally lose battles, the war has already been won for us! Jesus has defeated the arch-enemy of our souls, and walking with Jesus in daily discipleship is like marching in a victory parade.

In Luke's Gospel, chapter 10 was a success for the disciples. The seventy-two were sent out to preach. Given authority over the demons, they came back and said it had worked. And Jesus said, "I saw Satan fall like lightning from heaven" (10:18). He was so proud of them.

But in the chapter before, there had been a gigantic failure. It had to do with a demon-possessed child brought to the disciples by his father. The boy would scream, convulse, and foam at the mouth. The distraught father told Jesus, "I begged your disciples to drive it out, but they could not" (9:40).

Sometimes those early disciples failed miserably. At other times, they made their Lord proud of them. When they failed, he did not abandon them; when they triumphed in some notable way, he congratulated them. Through all their experiences, his message was this: "Don't give up because of your failures or become arrogant because of your successes. Don't even pay too much attention to the fact that demons react to my power through you. Rejoice instead that your names are written in heaven."

The same message needs to be heard by present-day disciples. Do you experience success and failure? Do your spirits soar on some days, only to crash in the depths on others? You must remember not to tie your spiritual security to your emotions. It rests on the saving work of Jesus rather than your feelings.

The ultimate outcome of the struggle between Jesus and evil was settled at the cross. There's where Satan was defeated. While the dark hours on the cross *appeared* to signal defeat for Jesus, they were the prelude to his resurrection on the third day. When he rose from the tomb, Satan's head was crushed (cf. Gen. 3:15) and he was disarmed (cf. Col. 2:15).

Since that day, there has been no doubt as to the outcome of the age-old struggle to which we are heirs and in which we have become participants. You and I are fighting a mopping-up operation for our Lord. I don't mean for this language to trivialize the struggles we go through. They are very real and very painful. Any victory we win gives God great pleasure, and Jesus rejoices with us in our successes. Even when we fail, however, it does not mean that the war has been lost. The war has already been won for us by Christ, and you and I simply march in his victory parade. "But thanks be to God, who always leads us in triumphal procession in Christ . . ." (2 Cor. 2:14).

The victory is not ours to win. It is ours to take as a free gift. We have been saved by grace, and salvation is God's free gift to us in Christ. When we understand this wonderful truth that the final outcome of heaven's war against evil is secured already, we begin to find the courage and strength to win more of our personal struggles against sin.

What is the Christian way for dealing with our fallen, sinful nature? Admit your powerlessness. Admit the fact that you are inadequate in your own resources and that there is no self-help methodology that will work for you. Throw yourself on Christ and ask for his fullness. Let him fill you with his Spirit to give you power. Let him transform you and make you anew in his image.

How do you deal with the matter of personal insufficiency? Give up the pretenses. Quit lying. Quit trying to act like everything is all right by wearing the mask of self-sufficiency. Confess Jesus for his all-sufficiency, and find your boldness in him. There's nothing that he can't cope with that's going to happen in your life. Once your insufficiency is admitted and the need to pretend is gone, Christ's all-sufficiency is your confidence. Christ will supply what you could never produce.

What about your uncertainties over the future? Nothing will happen in your life that Jesus cannot use to his glory. And death is no longer your great fear. We know our future is secure because Jesus triumphed over the grave.

Conclusion

The triumph most of us seek is the triumph of personal heroism, achievement, and honor. But the triumph of the Christian religion is that of another's deed. Christian righteousness is not attained but conferred. Salvation is not earned but received as a gift.

The war is over. We're just skirmishing in the hinterlands. Every fight is important. Every victory is precious. But even our losses can't be disastrous because our Savior has triumphed. And we are promised a share in *his* victory. We will participate in *his* celebration.

The war has been won. Be grateful. Rejoice. Believe that your salvation is a free gift of God's grace through your sometimes-faltering faith. Believe that God's sufficiency is great enough for your insufficiency. Rejoice, and be glad. Though you may be bandaged, bleeding, and wounded, you are marching behind Jesus in his victory parade of the saints.

For Reflection and Discussion

1. How pervasive is the analogy of *conflict* in the New Testament as a description of the Christian life? Find some metaphors in addition to the ones cited in this chapter.

2. Under what image does Luke present this conflict? Where does the struggle reach its climax? What event guarantees victory to Christ's followers?

3. How does the third Gospel present Christ's personal struggle with Satan and the demons?

4. What was the phenomenon of demon possession? Who could be taken captive by demons? What sorts of behavior marked those captive souls?

5. What did the success of his disciples against the demons demonstrate?

6. Explore the meaning of the debate between Jesus and his critics in Luke 11. Focus on the wider significance of 11:21-23.

7. If Christ has defeated Satan, why is there so much evil still present in the world? Why is life sometimes so difficult?

8. Identify the three areas of ongoing spiritual struggle named in this chapter. Define each. Illustrate each.

9. Show how Christ has supplied the means to victory in all three areas of human struggle named in question 8.

10. In your opinion, what is the primary obstacle to Christian *confidence* in salvation? What can be done to address it?

Chapter 12

Gloomy Gus Was Not an Apostle

What is a Christian supposed to look like? It is a serious question, and I hope you will walk through a mental experiment with me to try to visualize a Christian.

If you wish, include some of the more irrelevant features of the person you are imagining. Race. Color. Sex. The cut of clothes or neighborhood where you find him. Perhaps you even want to imagine an age.

Now try focusing on the face. Visualize the eyes. Eyes may be hard or pleasant. Accusing or accepting. Anxious or serene. Even sometimes tearful. Picture the mouth. It may be drawn or relaxed. Sad or smiling. Angry or peaceful.

The proper countenance for a Christian is one which reflects a soul who is secure, peaceful, and radiant in his Lord. Not an inane "smiley-faced Pollyanna," but a joyous expression. Not a Gloomy Gus who sees only the worst in circumstances and people.

The early church was a joyous church, and part of our task in restoring authentic faith in our day is to recapture that positive spirit. It's hard to rejoice when you feel like the world is falling apart. It's hard to be joyful when you think the weight of the whole universe has come crashing down on you in a moment. But we will learn shortly that joy is a larger concept than excitement or laughter.

The joy offered to Christians grows out of faith. And you can be sure your faith needs revitalizing when you have no more purpose and hope to your life than the non-Christian with whom you work. When you feel more confusion than confidence about right and wrong. When you discover that you are greeting life with clenched teeth and a frown. God would have his people face life with a faith radiant enough to produce joy where others might well give way to despair.

A typical dictionary definition of *joy* calls it "the emotion of great delight or happiness caused by something good or satisfying." I understand that definition and suspect it reflects current usage. Viewed this way, joy is when you land the big account you've been going for. It's when your chest swells out with pride as your son or daughter marches across the stage and graduates. It's being there to see your new grandchild for the first time. It's leading someone that you've prayed about and studied with for years to the Lord Jesus.

But does that definition of joy exhaust the biblical meaning? Does it do justice to the idea as it is found in the Word of God? Here is a text that makes me suspicious: "Consider it pure joy, my brothers, whenever you face trials of many kinds, because you know that the testing of your faith develops perseverance" (Jas. 1:2-3).

As used in Scripture, joy is an inner satisfaction which is larger than one's circumstances. Unlike the dictionary definition cited above, it does not grow out of good and satisfying events but may have to carry you through bankruptcy, a divorce, or a terminal illness. In the Bible, joy signifies a Spirit-given confidence about life which is greater than today's events.

The relevance of this theme and the need for this quality of life struck Luke with enough force that he deemed it important to make it one of his "selling points" in presenting the Jewish Messiah to the larger Gentile world to which he originally wrote.

Luke's View of the Christian Religion

In commenting on the theology of the third Gospel, one European scholar has written: "No other evangelist or

140

writer in the New Testament deals so often with the idea of joy as Luke." Though others treat the theme, he "far surpasses every other New Testament writer in the *frequency* with which he refers to the word 'joy.' "[1]

On Reicke's view, Luke's theology of joy is rooted in a sense of expectation. That is, Luke's Gospel demonstrates confidence in God. Looking to the arrival of the Kingdom of God, there is reason to rejoice no matter what is happening around Christians at the moment. Thus Luke's intention was "to emphasize again and again that the presence of grace in Jesus and in the gospel gives rise to *enthusiasm* at the thought" that God's purposes are unfolding.[2]

The pagan religions that Luke would have known in the Greek world of his day were superstitious, fatalistic, and ritualistic. They constituted such a confusion of beliefs and values that the world created by them was awash in uncertainties. They had no power, no sense of destiny, and no joy.

By contrast, Luke saw Christianity as the religion of truth, certainty, and purpose. It was filled with dynamism and characterized by joy. Luke thought it was important that Christians discover something that would provide them a settled sense of security that would be more dependable than the circumstance of the moment. He wanted believers to sense a security grounded in the faithfulness of God.

Joy as a Theme in the Third Gospel

The coming of the Savior was cause for rejoicing and singing. There is no better way, in fact, to establish the positive tone of Luke than to examine three songs in the opening two chapters. All three relate to the birth of Jesus and praise God for taking decisive action on mankind's behalf in sending his Son.

[1]Bo Reicke, *The Gospel of Luke*, trans. Ross Mackenzie (Richmond, VA: John Knox Press, 1964), p. 77.
[2]Ibid., p. 78.

Mary's song (1:46-55) is usually called *The Magnificat* and is so named for its first word in the Vulgate (Latin) version. With clear similarities to Hannah's song (cf. 1 Sam. 2:1-10), Mary sang in it of her exaltation by God's mercy from lowliness to greatness. One gets the impression that the song envisioned her own exaltation as typical of what comes to everyone who participates in the new order of things her child's birth would inaugurate.

> His mercy extends to those who fear him,
> from generation to generation.
> He has performed mighty deeds with his arm;
> he has scattered those who are proud in their
> inmost thoughts.
> He has brought down rulers from their thrones
> but has lifted up the humble.

Next is the song of the angels which proclaimed the birth of Jesus to shepherds in the fields near Bethlehem (2:14). The original angel who appeared told of the child who was born to be Savior, Christ, and Lord (cf. 2:11). With remarkable literary skill, three titles are braided together to form a strong cord. In Caird's words:

> The new-born baby is proclaimed to be Saviour, Christ (Messiah), and Lord. Saviour was a title with universal appeal. . . . and Luke knew that the promise of a Saviour would always command a hearing. As Messiah, Jesus would bring the hopes of Israel to fulfillment, as Lord he would summon the Gentile world to obedience and faith.[3]

Then comes Simeon's song (2:29-32) when the child was presented at the temple in connection with Mary's purification ceremony. Simeon was an old man waiting for the "consolation of Israel" (2:25), a rabbinic term for the

[3]G. B. Caird, *The Gospel of St. Luke* (London: Penguin Books, 1963), p. 61.

messianic age. He had been assured that he would live to see the Messiah. When he saw the infant with Mary and Joseph, he recognized him as the one born to be Messiah, praised God, and prophesied that the babe would be both "a light for revelation to the Gentiles and for glory to your people Israel."

All three of these beautiful songs are filled with praise. Each sounds a note of rejoicing. They combine to say that the coming of Jesus into the world was cause for singing.

Not only the birth but also the ministry of Jesus was an occasion of great joy. Following the healing of a paralyzed man by the Son of Man, both the man healed and the witnesses to his healing "gave praise to God" (5:25-26). When he raised the dead son of a widow of Nain, people "praised God" and said that the presence of Jesus was proof that "God has come to help his people" (7:16). After he healed a woman who had been crippled for 18 years, she "praised God" (13:13).

Once Jesus healed ten lepers who pleaded for him to have pity on them (17:11ff). One of them, a Samaritan, "came back, praising God in a loud voice" (17:15). Jesus then went to some lengths to affirm the appropriateness of that man's actions. Finally, the healing of a blind man at Jericho had the double effect of causing both him and a host of people who saw the miracle to praise God (18:43).

Again and again, Luke goes to great lengths to show that the presence and work of Jesus among men caused great excitement. Indeed, his Gospel ends on a note of joy and praise. After his account of the ascension, he closes the book with these words: "Then [the apostles] worshiped him and returned to Jerusalem with great joy. And they stayed continually at the temple, praising God" (24:52-53).

All this emphasis on joy, praise, and celebration is grounded in the notion that God is vitally concerned about

143

his creatures (cf. 15:6-7, 9-10, 22-24). Greek religions saw God as so high and holy that humans could scarcely come to his attention. Only the occasional "achiever" was worthy of divine notice. In Christ, however, Luke saw a God who knows us. Who identifies with us. Who saves mankind by personal sacrifice.

If you come to see God in terms of his personal concern for you, you can be happy on the darkest of days. Believe that Jesus died for you, and it will hardly be possible for you to think that he would abandon you in your present time of distress. This is a type of joy which runs deeper than the momentary thrill of some great achievement.

The Hunger for Happiness

We human beings are caught up in an unending quest for peace, joy, happiness, and meaning. God has planted this desire within us. It is not satisfied with money, one-night stands, power, or achievements. People trying to find life in these death-dealing settings become frustrated, confused, and angry.

God did not create a yearning for happiness without supplying its satisfaction. We are not condemned to be disappointed.

Remember the world Luke encountered? Life was a dog-eat-dog affair. It was seen as essentially pointless. There was little sense of joy or security. The world of our own day is the same. To use the language of our time, it is a struggle for survival and only the strong will survive.

The religions of Luke's day did not help very much to add joy and purpose to life. The god of some religions was so remote and distant as to be irrelevant; the god of others was so enmeshed with the world that he was trivial. Again, history repeats itself on this point in our own time. Some interpretations of God nowadays put him at a safe distance through reducing religion to ritual; others make him into a micromanager who is preoccupied with setting out the minutiae of their lives in everything.

How to Find Joy

How would someone set about to discover the sort of joy Luke considered so important? Here are five insights into the matter. Each relates to the kind of joy that does not depend on your external circumstances. It is a deep and settled peace with God. It is the sort of joy that survives the darkest day anyone will ever live.

Live guilt-free. Guilt is the great destroyer of joy. When I was 11 or 12 years old, I used to chase pigeons off the roof of a two-story building just down the street from my dad's store. The first floor was used by the Methodist Church, and the second floor was the meeting place for the town's Masonic Lodge. Pigeons used to roost right along the peak of the second story, and it just seemed my calling in life to keep them scattered by sailing rocks in their direction.

One afternoon I was heeding my calling. A handful of rocks was ready. The birds were in view. So I wound up and let fly. As one of the rocks began to fly from my hand, I knew something was wrong. It just didn't feel right. The angle was too low, and it was going to crash through a stained glass window on the second floor! I didn't even wait to see it hit. I just turned and ran. Over my shoulder, I heard the awful sound of glass breaking. I nervously finished my chores in Daddy's store and went home to dinner. Not much appetite that night. Not much sleep either. And not much sleep the night after that one.

What was I to do? Could I go on with my secret guilt? There was one man in the little town of Middleton that I knew to be both a Methodist and a Mason. So, after two sleepless nights, I made my way to the post office. There were no letters to mail, but I did have a confession to make.

Mr. Lester Simpson, the man with the double connection to my deed, was our postmaster. I told him the sordid, terrible story. Then I took all the money I had been able to get together out of the pockets of my jeans and laid it on his counter. For the first night in three, I slept. Guilt just won't let you have joy.

While Buddhism offers the snuffing out of desire and Islam demands achievement as the basis of salvation, Christianity offers you the merit of another who has paid sin's price for you. It allows you to deal with the problem of personal sin and its resulting guilt with divine forgiveness. You can be at peace with God through Jesus Christ. Because he has given his life for you, you can live guilt-free based on grace rather than merit.

Learn that problems are a part of life. Too many people are committing suicide these days, and a great many of those people are quite young. Suicide is the third leading cause of death among adolescents. Could it be that they've been led to expect life is supposed to be without pain?

A lot of marriages fail today. Could it be that some people get married with the assumption that everything is going to be "just right" and there will not be any problems? Could this be why so many marriages end within the first year after the wedding ceremony?

I think a lot of us have been sold a bill of goods about life in general. About marriage and careers in particular. The lie we have accepted insists that life just isn't supposed to be difficult. "Man born of woman is of few days and full of trouble" (Job 14:1). Your initiation fee into the club called humanity is challenge, problems, and heartache.

Very few people will enjoy perfect health. Not everybody will have an idyllic marriage, and nobody will have perfect children. (Children bear their parents' genes!) Everybody's work will have its periods of intense stress. On and on the listing of life's challenges could go. Some people thwart the possibility of joy in their lives by living with a harmful myth that says they have a right to expect to live above struggle.

Choose to be happy. Much of the misery we experience is because we choose to be miserable. We make a decision to put the bleakest possible interpretation on situations. We exploit them for their miseries.

The mother of a friend of mine illustrates how one can choose to be happy in a difficult situation. The only time I ever saw her was when she was lying in state just before her funeral. But I will never forget the story that Sellers Crain told during a eulogy at her funeral. Mrs. Rochell suffered from a severe, crippling form of arthritis in the last several years of her life. She had to give up housekeeping and go into a nursing home under constant care.

Sellers told about the first time he visited Mrs. Rochell after she had to go into the nursing home. Her body was already drawn and her hands were gnarled so that she couldn't do things that had always been important to her. Sellers said that he asked her, "Mrs. Rochell, do you think you're going to like it here?" To which she replied: "I came here to like it."

You choose what to make out of the circumstances of your life. You can choose to be miserable with much more than most people have, or you can choose to be happy with considerably less than you would like. Being happy is fundamentally a choice you make as to what you're going to focus on in your experience.

If God's own son had to live a less-than-ideal set of circumstances in this world, why should we think it unfair that we do? If he didn't have a place to call his own, suffered slights from friends, and became a victim to injustice, why is it so unthinkable that the same things could happen to his disciples?

Be involved with life. You can make a difference in the world by your presence in it. Show the way out of confusion's fog by living by the right principles and clear teachings of the Word of God. You can commit yourself to living in the holiness of Christ, and your life can make a difference in this world for Christ's sake.

Arlene Limas won an upset victory in taekwondo at the 1988 Olympic Games in Seoul, Korea. The 22-year-old American college student was standing on the center platform during the awards ceremony, wearing her gold medal around her neck. The stars and stripes began to go up. But the tape machine broke, and there was no national anthem. Bewildered about why the music wasn't playing, she began singing *The Star-Spangled Banner.* Then some people in the huge gymnasium joined her. Her parents. GIs in the stands. Within a matter of seconds, an athlete had become a conductor and was moving her arms up and down to lead the crowd in an *a cappella* performance of the national anthem.

This same sort of thing happens when someone has the courage to stand for what is right, takes steps to care for homeless people, or challenges a church to take its responsibility of evangelism seriously. People who get involved and dare to sing are often surprised by the other voices which join the chorus. Standing along the sidelines of life wringing one's hands changes nothing.

Learn that love is a verb before it's a noun. Most everyone believes that love makes life better, more secure, and more bearable. Our mistake, however, is in a romantic view which thinks of love as a noun. An abstraction. A remote ideal. In the Christian scheme of things, love is not an abstract notion. It became personal and practical in Jesus. He showed us that love is a verb before it's a noun. It is feeding hungry people and touching sick ones. It is bringing the confused and lost to an awareness of the Father who wants to save them.

Love is characterized by Paul in 1 Corinthians 13. Love is being kind to someone, perhaps even an enemy. Love is being gentle when you are tempted to deal harshly. Love is believing the best about other people. Love is pressing on when things are difficult

In a marriage, love is being patient, trusting, and kind. With children, it is not turning away if a son gets into trouble with the law or if a daughter gets pregnant. Before God, it is honoring him and obeying his word.

Conclusion

It has been my misfortune to know several people who were going to be happy *someday*. When they got better jobs. When they lost weight. When they got married (or divorced!). When they finished their education. Got the big promotion. Saved up some money. Got well.

On the other hand, it has also been my lot to know several people like Mrs. Rochell. People who found joy in spite of unrealized hopes and dreams. These noble souls seem to have believed that, if they couldn't be happy in their present situation, no change of circumstances would alter things enough to make them happy. Surely they were right, because happiness is more a matter of attitude than surroundings.

If you decide to let life's fluctuating circumstances dictate your level of joy, some days will be impossible. But if you link your peace, security, and happiness to one who is the same yesterday, today, and for ever, his abiding joy will see you through whatever may come.

Your personal worth and the meaningfulness of your life are affirmed by Christ. Your redemption has been purchased by him. Every promise that he has ever made to his people will be kept. No matter what your health condition. The size of your bank account. Or the other fickle elements of human life.

No, Gloomy Gus was *not* an apostle. And the presence of a Gloomy Gus or a Doleful Dorothy among his disciples today is a poor witness to the world. A failure of faith. An inconsistency.

Luke saw the presence of joy among believers as a magnet to unbelievers. It functioned just that way in the earliest days of the church. It will serve the same end when we exhibit it among ourselves today.

For Reflection and Discussion

1. What does the word *joy* mean? Is there a difference in today's popular use of the term and its biblical use?

2. Reflect on Bo Reicke's account of Luke's sense of joy. Does it make sense to you? Does it open a path to our own affirmation of joy in Christ?

3. What was the tone of the pagan religions of the first century? How was Christianity a welcome alternative to their mood?

4. Study the three songs which appear early in the Gospel of Luke. Identify the special emphasis of each one.

5. Trace the theme of celebration and praise through Jesus' ministry as chronicled in the Gospel of Luke.

6. What does *guilt* do to the possibility of spiritual joy? How has Jesus Christ met our need in this regard?

7. Show how unreasonable expectations can abolish joy. Is anyone's life free of trouble? What does the Bible say?

8. In what sense is happiness a matter of choice?

9. Contrast *cynicism* and *involvement* as ways of dealing with life's challenges. Can you cite an example of where someone's courage to act made the difference for others?

10. Read through the traits of love mentioned in 1 Corinthians 12:4-7. How do these behaviors bring joy to a life?